HOW TO: GET YOUR GAME UP

The Art of Social and Professional Communication Skills and Behaviours

By Beverley Law

Get Your Game Up

Copyright © 2014 Beverley Law

All rights reserved. No part of this publication may be reproduced, stored in a retrieval system or transmitted in any form or by any means, electronic, mechanical, photocopying, recording or otherwise, without the prior written permission of the publisher.

The information, views, opinions and visuals expressed in this publication are solely those of the author(s) and do not reflect those of the publisher. The publisher disclaims any liabilities or responsibilities whatsoever for any damages, libel or liabilities arising directly or indirectly from the contents of this publication.

A copy of this publication can be found in the National Library of Australia.

ISBN: 978-1-742844-63-3 (pbk.)

Published by Book Pal
www.bookpal.com.au

*Dedicated to my beloved Mark, Susan, Jerry, Aunty May, Sage & Quinn – how I loved you so.
...and for E.E. & C.W – who never knew how much I loved them, and for how long; in silence.*

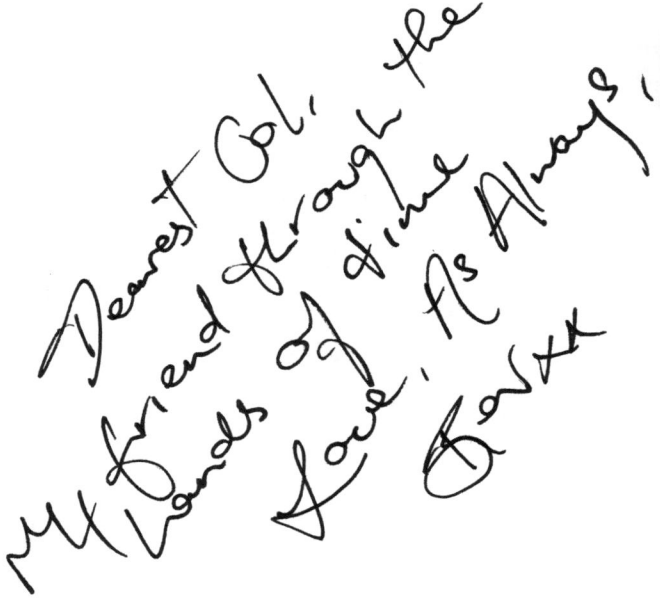

Contents

CHAPTER 1	MINDSET	1
CHAPTER 2	BODY LANGUAGE	14
CHAPTER 3	TALK LANGUAGE	56
CHAPTER 4	ETIQUETTE	70
CHAPTER 5	SOCIAL INTERACTION	77
CHAPTER 6	DATING/LOVE	98
CHAPTER 7	THE WORKPLACE	131
CHAPTER 8	THE SOUL & SPIRIT	137
SILENT CHAPTER: ANCIENT CIVILISATIONS		166
CHAPTER 9	YOUR ROLE	189
CHAPTER 10	THE ENIGMA	196
CHAPTER 11	LIFE'S SECRET ELIXIR	199
CHAPTER 12	EPILOGUE	201

PRELUDE: The Ministry of Behaviour / Doctrine Behaviourale

Well nothing like a thunderstorm to knock an old tree onto your new roof and hold the electrical cable hostage. Don't want to get electrocuted, hope my fish are still alive when the power comes back on. Need the air pump to filter in oxygen but the power company says if the power is not switched off I might get zapped. Sorry fish. Thinking this is where 'the rains it pours' saying came from. No jokes - how boring it is in the dark with no sound, no nothing, minimal light – it's all about me. How did those earlier civilisations survive?

One minute I was excited and talking on the phone to Aviary-Builder-Jeff, walking home from the bus stop after work and the next minute came around the corner, and thought there was clearly something different about my house. There I am talking to AB-Jeff and next minute calling the power company and putting my house on the life and death emergency call list. Truly if the wind kept blowing that heavy a$$ tree, and the taut power line broke – Zaptown for sure. (Thursday 6pm).

Thinking this was the perfect time to start this book, I had not one other thing to do there in the silent dark. Silence is a very powerful thing. Got a new computer but it's not charged so I'm writing in this chunky notebook (I think the cover's made of rock). Ordinarily in the past it would be my first reaction to panic and admittedly I did have, however brief, a moment of gasping out loud. Brutal life lessons have taught me that if there's nothing that can be changed in over, or even reacting, to a situation – then that's about the end of that gig. I 'do nothing' now and move on to something else...boring me in the dark.

14 hours and counting..." Yeah hello I have already reported my emergency but I'm calling back to say the electric line has started making a humming noise – should I even be here?" They told me to stay in case of a fire.

28 hours and counting.. I call for the third time now. She says I 'have to show patience during this trying time'.

"Hey thanks for coming." (Saturday 4pm)

"Wow this is really serious – how long has it been like this" - he says

"Uh- since Thursday"

"Why didn't you call and put your name on the Life and Death Emergency Call-Out List; this could have killed someone."

"That's the list I was on".

"Oh no you should have told them it was a life and death emergency situation"

"I thought the Life and Death Emergency Call-Out list covered it?"

"No you would have been upgraded to a Category Two – you're a Four. If I cut the power line the tree's going to go through your roof."

"Ah yeah I got that. Can you not just switch it off or something? My fish are already floating - the wood chopper wouldn't touch the tree till you switched off the main source ... I was a four all this time?"

The light at the end of the tunnel was a big freight train headed my way. My relative called and her best friend was diagnosed with ovarian cancer. Suddenly my broken roof, floating fish and lack of light seemed weak in comparison to her weekend.

Monday the girl at the cafe told me she had the "worst weekend" as her 'boyfriend's dogs got out in the storm and they struggled to find them'.

"Did you find them? Yes? I had a tree fall on the power line to my house and had to stay home in the dark in case the house caught fire" (like I would do something other than perish if that happened).

'Oh... your story beats my story" the café girl said.

"And I know someone whose beats both of ours."

There's always a story that beats your story. Always.

If you have chosen to read this book – is it because you think you could be better? Did someone give it to you because you need to be better? Are there opportunities you may have gotten if you performed better/spoke better/knew better? Acted differently?

Everyone stands to improve – some just choose not to and go about their way, attracting the same circumstances, repeating the same actions, getting the same results. Then again there are others, others who strive to learn, strive to be better, to have the advantage others have – they seek lessons from which others have grown. We sometimes think we would rather live our lives in someone else's shoes – who's to say those shoes will fit...and what if you have to travel the same path to earn those shoes, a path unseen & unheard – and one of much pain which is not reflected years down the road; pains long disguised or put to a far reach of the mind where one does not have to live with it daily. You have your shoes and they fit perfectly – make the most of the shoes you have on.

At the end of this doctrine you will be taught Charm, Body & Talk Language, Etiquette, Social Skills and

The Human Condition. You will be told 'Life's Secret Elixir'. If you utilise the information in this book you will feel and behave better, be better received and live an overall more rewarding life. If you read and disregard the information contained herein; know that an opportunity for change came your way – written in black & white, and you still did not take it...and then carry on with life as you have always known it to be. And so shall it be.

For those who seek to change their footprint...

Know that your whole life can change in the next two minutes. A mother who has lost a son or daughter will tell you in a miner's minute. Don't wait to find that out. Live your life like any or all of it could turn on a dime. The price of love is grief; death, divorce, distancing – that will never change. Beginnings must have an end. All things pass. Appreciate the things and people you have, in the time you have them. Be kind to those around you – you never know when someone's life will not run its full course. You should also learn to appreciate yourself for all you're worth and you must be worth it if the creator made you. Someone (or something) already thinks you are worth it – You're here.

No jokes it took a second thunderstorm for me to get back into the swing of writing this book.

It's howling down with two trees fallen (thankfully this time no major damage) and I haven't been motivated for a long time - busy with work and just living life – that takes up enough time as it is. That's the same excuse for all of us isn't it? Don't have the time. It takes effort and one has to make the time for self-improvement.

Fear - it's such an arbitrary thing really isn't it. Life can be a bit that way. Wanting to alter the outcome of a certain path or mindset, of which the end result is already predetermined. We seek change for things that simply are destined to play themselves out to the end, and all the fuss and worry in the world won't change the course of events due to take place. The only thing that ever holds one back is Fear.

This is to "Get Your Game Up on a Whole"...

People fix certain parts of themselves – the really obvious areas that require changing. Posture is a good start. Don't look down – good eye contact. Cool, calm exterior and conversations. But it's not enough. One must fix the unit as a whole, and that involves all aspects of it. A repairman fixing a white good wouldn't fix a part of the motor; if he was pulling it apart - he would check that all parts of the motor were in good working order, at least a good repairman would. That is the aim of this doctrine – Some areas you may be well versed in and not so much in others, you now have the opportunity to become Well-Rounded. Seek out and make the changes required in you; to make sure you have the maximum game on at any time you call upon it. If you've made mistakes – don't let them steer the rest of your life. Make the commitment to change today, in this moment of time. Don't make excuses. The change is upon you.

Declare a new day.

CHAPTER 1   MINDSET

I used to complain about having no shoes till I met a man with no feet.

Mexico

There are animal trainers who say 'the most important thing is the energy we give off'. If animals can pick up our energy so readily – what would stop humans from following suit? Martial Arts teach you the same thing – it is the energy you give off, the chi that flows within you is the giveaway visually of who you are and how you honestly feel about yourself. You can literally 'see it coming'.

Have you ever been in the company of a person who you meet and decide in an instant, you just don't like them, not that in your hasty assumption you gave them time to do anything to you. For whatever the reason, they just give off a vibe you don't like. And you don't like them. Or so you say. It might not be that you don't like them as much as you don't like what they do, how they act or, on a subconscious level, their vibe.

And then there'll be other times when you talk to someone for five minutes and feel like you've known them all your life? You've warmed to them instantly.

There's a reason people have those reactions and some people have mastered the ability, to activate that reaction whether with or without knowing it, to the positive or the negative.

Some of the most accomplished sales people I've met had a knack of making one feel that they are the only people in the world that matter. You must have heard that before. A very powerful tool of persuasion, and then on the other hand, I have met people who could turn you off just as soon as you look at them, or worse still, hear or smell them coming. Certainly they would do something about it if they knew of their power to repel.

My friend once, at the gathering of age old friends from high school; told the story of how her friend went to the hairdresser to change her way out look. The hairdresser said after '"Thank god for that - you looked ridiculous". Mia's friend exclaimed – 'why didn't anyone tell me'... "So this is me telling you" is how she ended that story with our black & white haired friend. It doesn't matter how you tell someone an important truth – just that you do, of course the kindest route possible is always the best, it's so they have an awareness and can go on to decipher whether it is something that needs changing. It affects their mindset. It affects yours. The truth is a general consensus & not your opinion alone. Sometimes you have to sit the truth out – any married man will tell you the truth is not to be mentioned when his wife asks:

"Do I look fat in this?"

"In this room – no you don't, but in that dress…well goodness me."

That man would be making himself comfortable on the couch possibly for all eternity if he ever came out with something like that. The truth is always warranted for you to sleep well at night and for you to live a peaceful and carefree life – it's just a matter of to what degree. I worked for a company whose motto was "There are no degrees of honesty". Either you are an honest person or you are not… nobody can be a little bit honest as that would also make them a little deceitful – hence, they can't be trusted as to which they would deploy under any given circumstance.

People can tell when you don't tell the truth, some people sense it and some people are trained in reading deception. One thing that can be said is that taking someone 'at face value' has a meaning most never knew existed. Know that if you change a story once – all of your other versions of events, no matter how small or insignificant, will come into question…and with micro expressions – you can't hide them if you tried. We will cover the basics of these in this book however if you are in sales or a related people person field, I strongly recommend you read up on it, separately and in depth. It will save you a lot of time; but it will make it hard to date you if you are single. Do you know you can tell a man is gay just by the tension in his face? Sitting on public transport and seeing men with wedding rings and that level of tension and I think; you are ripping yourself and someone else off if that is really what is inside you. One of my friends is married to a gay man only she doesn't know it and I wonder if he really does after fifteen years of martial denial. "He's in touch with his feminine side" she tells me after having relayed a particularly girly story about him. I want to say – 'ah, no, he's as gay as a carnival' – but that is one of those calls you leave for the Universe to address. Every mannerism he has is feminised and she likes that about him – 'Yeah, all Fag Hags do'. (any gay man will tell you that's a term of endearment). My childhood friend told me of his divorce, and the triggering factor was a line he read in a poem by D.H. Lawrence:

"A man who forces himself to love another, begets a murderer in his own body.

Live your life as who and what you really are. Be truthful above all else to yourself. You are after all the one that matters most. When you have the mindset and well-being of a person who lives an honest and forthright life, you really wouldn't have it any other way anymore. That inner harmony and sense of peace shines from within. But most importantly – you can't ever expect to find any lasting sense of happiness from actions that are not based in truth. I have addressed truth as a starting point just because you won't get far without it. If you don't like who you are - change it, but you must be honest with the starting point. Honest people are better people, all round. Even Shakespeare from way back when, knew enough to write "To thine own self be true." People who swear are, for the most part, regularly truthful.

Now regarding Mindset - How do you expect to convince someone else you're worth it if you don't think so yourself. "Hey I really want to sell you this _____ but if you ask me its lame" and then still expect the person to buy what you're selling. That is in essence what you are trying to pull off, whether you think it shows or not. A survey done by the Unilever/Dove group had results showing that "2% of women worldwide and 1% of Australian women think they are beautiful. That's quite telling as to how women really feel about themselves, when statistically we know these results can't possibly be true based on what women of the world actually look like."

First things first; you have to get a grip on who you are, what your weaknesses and strengths are (and Not the internet dating version either...the picture from 10 years ago etc.) Who are you? What did you become, are you the person you set out to be – did you get to where you're going? Take a wrong turn... what's your story and what do you Really want it to be?

Start the mental picture TODAY. You must see yourself living the life you always wanted instead of sending negative or mixed messages out into the Universe, for it to give you what you're telling it to do. I'll give you the 'heads up' on what not to say out loud: "How much worse can it get!". You will see a plethora of circumstances befall, that are only too happy to show you how much worse things can get.

If you weren't worth it I'm sure our creator in his infinite wisdom wouldn't have made you – so here we all are.

What we perceive as important changes from time to time, are for some people daily.

You get good at what you do time and again, even if it's negging yourself out. If you keep telling yourself you're 'not good at'... or you are 'not attractive' or whatever that internal voice tells you, that adds to the imprint of your mind and what it holds foremost, over the positive mindset and messages you are capable of.

Creative Visualisation: If you go about your life thinking you or it are shiet, then that is the creative picture you are putting into the Universe. You will live to see the life you see sub-consciously. We move toward what we picture in our mind. If you picture a dull existence you will be made to live it. Picture yourself contented – picture abundance, if you have monetary concerns – picture yourself happy and never worried about the universal flow of money. It comes freely to you. Mind you – if you are a real (expletive) then you have other stuff to sort out first before the Universe, in its absolute abundance, provides for you unabashedly. You weren't born in a vacuum from the outside world. How did you get this way and what external forces in life made you the way you are today? As it stands though, you can still be a better person, it just takes a little extra work is all. Let those behaviours no longer become you – in the truest sense of the words. Do it for yourself and your own future happiness. You can't ever expect good to come from bad intent, and yes you will pay back your experience tenfold. You know the moments of "Why me" – yeah – well that's what that's about. You will be made to feel everything another has been made to feel, by your actions. That goes for good too. Before one knows the laws of Karma it can take seven years to catch up, once you are aware of the nature and laws of karma, you'll be lucky if it can go seven minutes without getting the karmic beetchslap from hell. Any negativity you address or worry about sends the wrong picture into creation. Be kind to yourself and others, do all you can do to make the everyday interactions with people, whether strangers or not, an experience of which nothing but good comes. Thereby nothing but good will is returned to you. The seemingly bad experiences are put there to mould you into who you need to be, lessons are things that you may be lacking in, and they are to be taken as the growth experience for which they came. In a book called the Bhagavad-Gita, the worst circumstances that you are made to go through are called A Beautiful Mistake. Even death, is just a beautiful mistake and in that mistake of the person being taken from you too soon, lies the growth and lessons you will then be forced to learn, to perhaps show a deeper level of appreciation - which will bring forth the beauty in your life. One needn't allow the experiences to make them victims but more so, opportunities one has been given to grow. Outlook is everything for healing and progression in life.

As of this moment start the beginning of the new you. Right this second you no longer play that negative soliloquy in your head that tells you 'You can't do that'.. 'You're not good enough for this'. Your Permanent Positive Mindset starts here. Now. You are no longer the person you were even 5 minutes ago. Everything about you and the patterns you created in the past are different. From the next time you stand up – stand tall and don't look down. Pretend there is a string going from the tip of your head down your spine to your tailbone. That is the body language posture you need to carry visually for others to perceive you as confident and assertive, whether you are the slightest bit inclined to be (it's only temporary for now if you are not). Looking down all the time insinuates uncertainty about oneself. Even if you are uncertain about yourself; no-one needs to know it from afar any more.

"My Cup Overfloweth" – That's what I say when someone asks how I'm doing. It could be the furthest thing from pay dirt... the worst sequence of events in one morning, whatever – feeling the lowest in two months, and I'll still say "My cup overfloweth" regardless of whether I drowneth in my cupeth that day. It may take a few days or more but something will happen that makes me think: I am most fortunate and my cup really does overflow. Albeit; one can get some days when the cup overfloweth so much so you think you might drown in the quagmire... But "this too shall pass". It could be perceived as nagging the Universe but no. One gets all that they ask for that won't turn their life upside down. I look back at the things I've asked God for and I am thankful that at least one of us was thinking about my best interest, and looking past the next thirty minutes.

You may have noticed already, I have taken a page out of Shakespeare's book and if I can't express what I need to enough in the literary word, well I'll just make a word up. If Wills can do it, so can I. And while I'm at it - I have chosen to sporadically repeat, instead of inserting some important messages into only one chapter – this is a strategy for implanting into memory.

This creative visualisation stuff is old hat and for most people unbelievable, but if you want to make change; one must first do it in the mind. We move towards what we want most in our mind. Ask any Criminal profiler. If you haven't finely tuned your thought processes correctly, everything else will be an uphill struggle. So we start here first:

Concentrate – Visualise: Picture the world you see yourself in at your most successful. Picture your dreams come true. Feel the joy of winning that award, that accolade, that gold medal whatever it is you aspire in the dreams you dream for yourself – these things you know would make you happier. Studies show that the human mind absorbs what is fed to it. On a BBC documentary about the mind, a gymnast who had difficulty doing the triple turn in the air (whatever they call that in gymnastics) could not succeed until she worked her mind into doing it smoothly. By creatively visualising herself successfully doing the act and the joy of having succeeded in performing this manoeuvre, only then did the woman actually accomplish the task at hand, and she did so with ease. Get it in your head that You Are - THE BEST OF THE BEST AND THE BEST OF THE REST. You are worthy. The qualities you have and hold are duplicated by no other. The only thing that stops you is you. We tend to be our own Hiroshima's, a mighty bomb that can go off causing wrack and ruin to all around – a private or personal menace of sorts. You owe it to yourself to give yourself the best chance at happiness available to you and to stop self-sabotaging your attempts to succeed. The first thing one has to knock off is the verbal monologues in their head.

As of today you should start to reset your verbal clock. The voice inside your head that says 'I can't, I'm not' - should as of this day forth turn into the "**I**

am" monologue. Additionally, the "What if…" monologue is just as damaging. So too, "If but for…"

'I am witty and fun to be around – I am smart and confident – I am' … you get the picture… everything you think you need to be better at and are not. As of today you already are. If you can control your mind you can control your body. If you convince yourself mentally you are witty and confident in a new crowd or work related setup - see if your palms don't sweat less. The only 'I am not' you should entertain is I am not nervous of meeting new people... I am not stupid and make a good impression. However you really should take the negatives out of it altogether. You have to change the way your mind perceives yourself and in this new methodology – your mind will be retrained to reinstate the changes, just as you have convinced yourself otherwise. It is about setting yourself free from all the old cr@p you've told yourself and resetting a positive mindset. Think and recite in the positive only.

There are different strategies very effective people take from writing notes and sticking them on their mirror, fridge etc. If this prompts you to better keep the changed messages, so be it – do what suits you best; whether that means recording these messages to audio for them to be listened to whilst on the way to work, or just saying them in your mind, it is not important how you do it, just that you do. The only person that can stop you from moving forward now is you. You can start with the mental chant "All is well" if you can't think of any to begin with.

Music: What you listen to is the mood you carry. Mozart, Chopin, Heavy Metal. When you listen constantly to a loud thumping bass noise with negative lyrics your mindset follows suit. Heavy metal enthusiasts can be found to be quick to anger, have excessive use of darkened clothing etc... it all results in a pattern that is not conducive to Harmony shall we say. Whereas if you listen to calm, melodic music, your mindset follows suit. You never hear of a professional sports person listening to heavy metal music before going out to play an important match; they may be setting themselves up to crash and burn unless in the boxing arena. Roger Federer, the tennis pro mediates and listens to calming music before a game and it isn't to Megadeath or Poison. There are numerous books written about the effect of music on the soul and psyche, as well as plant growth.

Snowflakes have one quintillion molecules (100 trillion trillion) Experiments have been done with ice crystals – the experiment played different types of music while the water was freezing. The softer slower music formed shapes, clearly visible under magnification, flower like soft, rounded harmonious/gentle looking shapes. The heavy metal music formed a spiked pattern – a shredded and stabbing appearance. Do try this at home. Since our body is made up of such a high density of water, it seems only course that the music has the same effect on us.

You never see a brawl break out in a room where the artist is playing the flute, (nor in a room full of potheads incidentally). If you don't have a microscope and aren't that eager - This same differentiation occurs when music is played near sand molecules; in a layer on a flat surface, the softer and more harmonious the music, the more fluid the pattern it makes.

As with everything in this book – you needn't take my word for it. For example, there are books on water/snowflake/sand patterning that explain it as such, as is with every other topic addressed herein – it is your call whether to read up on things that you may think unrealistic or wish to have a greater knowledge about. This is about your expansion. I am only telling you of things learned and am shortcutting for you.

Think as if it's already happened – Act as if it's already here. Live It. Believe.

CHAPTER 2   BODY LANGUAGE

The body will not lie for you
Egypt

Watching at the table my friend was playing on at the casino & having noted only two guys in the whole house that did a good poker face - Kristine might as well have held her cards the opposite way. Don't know who she thought she was hiding them from. I even said 'you may as well just tell them you have a shiet hand,' like they couldn't see that from looking at her.

Body language training is the single most valuable tool in life. It takes approximately 4 minutes for a person to assess another in nearly 100% of cases – Body Language and Micro/Macro Facial Expression compose of up to 80% of this assessment. Your hygiene and clothes you wear are amongst things to take into account for the last twenty percent of an impression. It's the simple things, the things you have no control of that happen in a fleeting second. One can't cover the complexities in this book but it is ever so strongly recommended you research it yourself or it is addressed in depth at my workshops. Particularly if you're in business or sales especially, you will have much to gain. Be forewarned that you live a different life when you know the truth of the situation – you will not even need to hear the words being spoken to get a gist of, for example, the severity of a conversation. You just need to see a person's face or watch their feet (the single area people who master control of themselves forget about) regardless of what words are being voiced out loud, it is the actions expressed that enlighten you to what is really going on. The body and especially the face, speaks volumes. Even the shape of the face tells its own story about its wearer. For example a person with a Round face is often found to have good business and social skills; they are highly compatible with others with their relaxed nature. However, impulsive behaviour belies underneath the veneer of reliability and confidence. Other face shapes include Oval, Square, Conical and Triangular and they all speak volumes about a person with that face shape. As well, People with Triangular shapes are those one might find mostly in a creative field; whereas Square faced people are confident leaders. The Round belong to people with great energy – the life of the party. Additionally, there is type based on head shape: Square/Round/Egg-Shaped. This method of reading a person goes as far as ears, nose, eyes, eyebrows, forehead, and lips - it even goes as far as the distinct differences in the space between the lips and nose and the characteristics of those people. It doesn't matter which book on this topic one reads – they pretty much tell you the same thing for the signs. The characteristics of each sign stay the same whether it's from Desmond Morris's The Naked Ape written in 1967 to Charles Darwin's The Expressions of Emotions in Man and Animals from 1872. There's also Body Language for Dummies, Kuhnke wrote in 2007. Take your pick and if you read multiples of, you will soon see the messages are on par with each other. Body Language and the reading of it has been around a long time; but for some reason people are not aware of the benefits gleaned from the knowledge of learning this art form. This one tool and the practise of it will set you apart from others.

Handwriting Analysis and Body Posturing go hand in hand – how we move and our movement on paper is most telling. Additionally you can most often tell if a person is right handed or left handed, as their fingernails are usually shorter on their dominant hand.

You may have seen some Mentalists work. They are versed in the Art of Psychological Manipulation. They use subtle gestures to implant decisions into a person's subconscious. Without them being aware of it - they point to or refer, to implant into the subconscious what they want you to think. Their actions are picked up subconsciously. For example, they might ask of a person whether they refer to a boy or girl, stick figure or clothed, in a garden or an open field – all the while nodding yes and giving hand cues as to what they want them to think; and then the person is amazed that the mentalist knew they had in mind a stick girl in a skirt bouncing a ball in the garden, when in fact, that was the image implanted into the person's subconscious mind from the outset. This takes extensive practise and is detailed work - it is not addressed herein as there is always the chance that the knowledge may be used for something other than good. The subconscious is such a powerful aspect of the mind; one could cause havoc if this power was used effectively by the wrong person. There is no doubt hypnosis exists and some people in the study have shown that it can be used on large groups of people. If you examine the speeches of Hitler; you can almost see in the people he addresses, that a form of hypnosis has been used for the masses, standing in droves, fully compliant. In the Second World War high operatives were hypnotised with sensitive material, of which they didn't know themselves they had the knowledge of. On arriving at their designated location, the information was retrieved by the other cleared party using a code word to obtain it, and the hypnotised officer went on his way without ever knowing their minds held that knowledge. There are multiple books and practitioners of these subjects.

There are many aspects to Body Language (Kinesics), not least; one must look for behaviour "clusters" which are a group or combination of signals consistent to conclude one message, instead of isolated signals which can be misconstrued. Read signals in context e.g. room temperature/crossed arms. If the room is steaming hot and they have their arms crossed – this can be assessed as definitively, a negative blocking motion.

Consider ethnicity when you address personal space (Proxemics) guidelines state: Personal Space = 45-120cm/ Public = No interaction desired; 12ft plus. Western cultures have a lesser depth of personal space than do eastern cultures. Age also differentiates. Older women may exhibit modest showing of body language based on upbringing or the limitations brought on by clothing. A younger woman may be more obvious and easily read.

Kinaesthetics is physical movement and experience, the learning styles of which tangible action is not required. For example team building exercises unlock a person's potential using Kinaesthetics.

There are three sides to every human being as we know it – The Public Side: which we show to people outside, mostly people we don't know well or strangers. The Private Side: which is reserved for our family, friends and partners/spouses and our Secret Side: of which very few people ever know if any do. The reading of this and the next chapters will move us from a person's public side to private side in real time.

Once you have become familiar with the basic meanings of Body Language, it can be so easily read it jumps out at you. Predicting a way a person will behave in the future can be determined from their past behaviour – it's this subconscious patterning that shows future behaviour - by watching people and their modes of behaviour, they become predictable.

Darwin was one of the first to acknowledge 'universally recognised' facial expression as a result of evolution (nature), said he. Meaning these expressions are inborn and genetic to us, regardless of what part of the globe one is born. The other part being environmental (nurture) e.g. personal space is learned rather than genetically inherited.

We have actually been indulging in the world of body language since the dawn of mankind. If early man in a hunt saw a threat – his body language was easily conveyed to other members of the hunt without words (also body language of animals). We, today, can see signs of alarm in another human being and can make a run for it without words being spoken too. We have only in this century started using it as a tool for the workplace and other communications.

Women inheritantly pick up body language subconsciously more often and more easily than men; perhaps, it is said, from our ancestry of having to protect their lives and the lives of their children. As a part of course, women needed to be alert to whether the man meant harm or not. Most will acknowledge that this still applies today.

There is much detail in the study of Non-Verbal/Non-Vocal Communications however here you can get the basics you need to get by. In its most basic form; the body speaks for itself, under stress the body will give away more as the autonomic nervous system, which controls pulse and breathing amongst other things, cannot be controlled. It works independently from our will, as all else.

Open Body Language: Open body language in its most basic form is with legs and arms uncrossed, a posture of relaxation. Crossed arms simply state (when the temperature is not cold) – that the person you are talking to you is switched off from what you're saying. Look at the body's posturing in its most simplistic form – open body language is a cue to continue on with whatever you're trying to deliver, a good time in sales to try a Trial Close. Head nodding and mirroring of the person to your actions is subconscious agreement. Arms not contacting, not crossed – feet either crossed at the ankle or at knees. If a person's body looks like a barrier by their own body appendages – they are creating a block to the information being heard. A relaxed posture insinuates a relaxed mood. A slight slouch/arms open and not fixed closed – legs apart (not in the streetwalker way) When a man spreads his legs wide apart he is referring subconsciously to his sexual confidence. It is a 'look here' action.

Closed Body Language: Crossed arms and/or legs. There is a very simple way to unlock a person's folded arms so they stop blocking you out in what you are saying = Pass them a piece of paper with something on it as if they need to take a look at something, anything – it can be an object you pass. The one and only time you should consider continuing contact with a person with folded arms is if it is cold. Herein lays the very essence of why a cluster of signals is required. Everything else is a body block which all but says out loud "I'm not listening to you". It is a pseudo barrier to keep what is being received at bay and anything offered to a person in this stance is at best being ignored. Stop – undo their closed position and then continue on if you really want to be heard. When assessing body language look at it as a whole. It almost tells you what's going on if you look at it like a picture.

Mirroring: Opposites attract they say but 'like attracts like' in the end it is clear. If you want to build up and speed up repoire - the mirroring technique commonly used by sales masters, is a very successful procedure. If you were to cross your legs in one direction – the other person crossed theirs in the same direction, that person is in sync with you. If you study the body language of couples and people who already have feelings for each other – they mirror subconsciously. They are sitting or standing in the same stance. Mirroring is an art and a subtle one at that. If you are overt in these actions – whoever you are mirroring will think you're a nut. It is an appeal to the subconscious in that if someone was to lean back relaxed, you would assume the same posture however you may wait for a few minutes to elapse before slouching yourself ever so slowly or in small bursts to where you end up in the same stance. You are subconsciously telling them – 'I am like you'. With mirroring they will think 'we are the same'- people trust those who they think are like themselves. In a sales arena; this behaviour is imperative to getting the person in sync - before you ask them to buy your product.

Face Value: There is too much detail in the education of Micro and Macro Facial Expressions, there is much reading material on the facial expressions and what they represent. Easily recognisable are the standard Macros – Surprise / Anger / Fear / Happiness / Disgust / Sadness. The furrowed brow of concern – we innately know these and they are universally recognised regardless of race or cultural divides. Micro expressions are the ones we cannot control and happen in a short lived moment, as they are often the ones people attempt to disguise. Micro facial expressions are an area that is addressed in detail in my Sales-Master Training. Having met sales masters along the way – they inherently seem to know what a person is thinking and feeling. They can give the impression they know how a person feels or thinks – but they don't know anything other than what the person is subconsciously telling them from their own free will and facial giveaways. The true mastery of the micro facial expressions lies in one's ability to see the 'fleeting movement' – which is the hardest part of learning the technique involved in reading them. For maximum benefit here and now I will endeavour to enlighten you to the foremost emotion people want to detect = Deceit. This assists you in all aspects of your life, including your job.

Signs of Deceit/Lying: Facial twitch – covering the nose – eyes looking shifty - eyebrow movement – watch pupils of the eyes for dilation. Reactions of body language are uncontrolled motor responses.
Touching or scratching the nose (increased blood flow) or touching the mouth (different to touching the neck which is indicative of them not believing you) Looking down – no eye contact - licking lips. Sometimes you could be for example accusing a lover of cheating, if they smile, laugh or do any other inappropriate action – chances are they are not being forthright = the reaction has to be relevant to the question/situation. One commonly sees serial killers with a smirk they just can't hide when discussing how they have been unfairly accused. Review the tapes of Bill Clinton as he says he 'did not have sexual relations with Monica Lewinski'. He has a smirk on his face a great deal of the time about something that could cost him the Presidency of the United States – he knows subconsciously he's going to try and tell a helluva-lie and his face won't let him. Additionally, he touches his nose over twenty times. Another prime example that can be viewed, is the news stories of Susan Smith who drove her own car into a lake with both of her children in it and said 'a black man carjacked her'. She made that mistake (smirking) and another one that were most obvious – she over gave details in describing him. Knowing more detail or overdoing it – she went on about the

ribbing in his hat and seemed to know more as time went on in the sketching process, when indeed she should have been able to describe less and less. It didn't ring true to the officers. She has a smirk on her face every minute she stands in front of the camera begging the public for the safe return of her children which she, on both a conscious and subconscious level already knows they are not safe. You can lie with your mouth but your body cannot and will not, lie. Additionally; the upper lip curls upwards in disgust when someone is telling a lie is another way of detecting deception; as viewed on the news footage of an Australian killer, John Sharpe, who murdered his wife and child with a spear gun. Even he was disgusted by his own actions and couldn't hide it as much as he tried for the cameras. Genuine regret is shown by a pursing of the lower lip causing a dimple motion in the lower mid part of the mouth. An example of this is Colonel Oliver North when asked about his military role in Reagan's administration – he did regret his actions although he was attesting to having no feeling for what orders he had followed and what had taken place. Once these micro expressions are viewed one can place them almost immediately when seen. People will interlock their fingers when they have no intention of telling the truth or are pitching an idea they don't believe in. It will usually be in accordance with other negative body language signals. Far and away, the best practise for body language training is watching commercial advertising or a really bad TV drama. One can readily see with practise, who has never used the product or service, yet profess to swear by its effectivity. I have inserted these visuals for reference:

BITING FULL OR PART LIP – LYING – MICRO

OVEREMPHASISED OPEN GUESTURE – SMIRKING FOR SERIOUS TOPIC (IRAQ)

FURROWED BROW – INTERNALLY STRESSED/TIGHT LIPPED (STOPPING SELF)

CLOSED BODY LANGUAGE

INTERLOCKED FINGERS – NOT BEING FORTH-RIGHT/DECEPTIVE

SWEATING/OVEREMPHASISING/GUILT
REVERSAL – DECEPTIVE

WHAT MARILYN REALLY FELT INSIDE – (MI-CRO) R. Avedon

OH NO. – MACRO　　　　　MICRO

ANGER

DEVASTATION/REGRET – MICRO (unintended for others to see)

SUPRISE (SS) MACRO FACIAL EXPRESSION (the obvious, universally recognised)

RELATIONSHIP LANGUAGE: CLOSE BUT NOT
(Micro)

It's quite clear, which of these couples is the more in love of the two, based on the micro expressions having escaped subconsciously. Even though they know they are facing a camera they have not been able to stop the expressions from being released. That is the very nature of micro expressions; they cannot be altered by conscious thought.

Animals show emotions similarly according to Charles Darwin in "The Expressions of Emotions in Man and Animals" 1872 (Love)

There is only one known way to cheat on a polygraph test, one of the few detectors of deception; the rest of the time it's pretty much a fluke. Police can recognise if you have taken a certain relaxant medication and all the usual attempts. There is supposedly only 4% of the population that are so good at lying and deception that the best trained are hard pressed to read their faces. Most of them with psychopathic personalities and traits able to not disclose facial recognition signs – Perfect practise makes perfect. Perhaps a true psychopath who has convinced themselves of the lie can still avoid being exposed by the polygraph. Tell a lie long enough and it becomes a reality. Of course I'm unable to share the knowledge of cheating a test with you in this doctrine, however hopefully at the end of reading here you will not be the kind of person who ever has to sit one. Science has since made advances on detecting deception ranging from Brain Imagery to Computer Recognition of Micro Facial Expressions; slated to be used in the future at airports and the like.

When you live the right way and life follows an honest course – you'll never have to worry about such things. Know that the days of seeing clearly through deception are upon us. Habitual lying is a habit that experts say, is impossible to break. Para-renal is a study of the eyes – the eyes don't lie, and giveaways are in eye movements and lid tension.

Assessment is done by looking at the eyes – one can literally 'see it in the eyes'. A look to the left is a sign of looking into the past as in someone who is trying to reflect on the circumstances that occurred in an event whilst a look to the right, is indicative of someone looking to the future as in a situation that more likely did not occur and are trying to foresee how the story needs to be told. Truthful answers rarely have the person pause – always be alerted by someone pausing before answering a question. The truth doesn't change so it is repeated without concern the story may have changed. Furthermore, a breakdown of whether the look is upward/middle/or downwards has been studied. Upper is to an 'auditory' nature. Looking to the middle is reflective of a 'visual' personality and downwards shows one is dealing with an 'emotionally' driven nature. Practising viewing these movements and detecting them as a part of your own second nature, is particularly beneficial to people in the Sales or Public Relations fields although once practised, you will find it is also highly beneficial in a social field. Additionally, each person has one eye more open than the other. Right Brain Thinkers (Creative) have the left eye more open as do the Left Brain Thinkers (Analytical) have the right eye slightly bigger than their left. In the brain the right side affects left actions as is the opposite true, left side controls right side of the body. This combination assists one in sales for example – it is readily available knowledge for alerting one to the fact they have a Visual person (for example) whose sales direction would be to 'paint the dream'. "If you have this product/service and its benefits, you will be able to afford that house on the beach you dream of". It also becomes readily apparent if your client is being up front with you regarding their capabilities to afford or even want your service. Oftentimes, when in the course of an otherwise average conversation, throw in unexpectedly the question you really want answered, and the person caught off guard by the change in momentum, will blurt out the truth quite by accident. i.e. chit-chat, chit-chat "you really can't afford this product can you Gary?" – 'No my son is in college next year and we need the savings'. It's happened, it happened to me.

The average person lies approximately 4 times a day. This can be detected by the changes one notices in their body language, eyes and thoughts – a change in temperature (flushing) - increased chest expirations (the body is unable to relax when in the mode of lying) – Heightened anxiety cues are what one should be looking for when trying to detect deception. The autonomous system will be activated. These movements are quick and one needs to be focussed on the face and body to catch that glance away, subconscious shoulder shrug or fleeting raised eyebrow. Shaking the head a little too long in a No gesture is the opposite of honesty – they are trying too hard. A baseline of honesty needs to be obtained; which can be done simply by saying "what is your name?" or "you must be (Name)" – The average person is not going to lie about their name unless in a nightclub and avoiding you. When they answer – this is your baseline of what you now need to observe as anything different to or outside of. Predominantly, the most basic detection capacity is from having an appropriate response to the question: a man who has been caught cheating, knowing his marriage and children are on the line - should not have a smile on his face when denying the incident – or even a glimmer of a smirk. The response Must be relative to the question. The emotional response must be appropriate to the severity of the circumstances. It is the autonomous system that will force this smile. The pupils contract / corner of the mouth twitch / eyebrow lift – these will be fleeting so it is important for the cluster to verify truthfulness. Also, the voice lowers & deepens whilst being deceptive.

It's not like you can grab a stranger's wrist and feel their pulse racing, or touch their chest to feel their heart pounding out of it – so watching their face, body language and feet will be an imperative part of detecting deception. The feet are the most obvious sign, especially in attraction. If they are facing away from you – Not going to happen. People in deceptive mode often forget about their feet and it is often the quickest tell-tale sign of how an encounter is going. Especially if the person is putting on a brave front and their feet are shaking or unsettled underneath the table.

If you really want to upset all and sundry, there is a definitive process whereby you will see clearly how the body will not lie: Ask someone to tuck their thumb into a closed fist, pointing downwards. Have them stretch the arm outwards away from the body in a straight line to the shoulder. You would then place two fingers underneath their upper arm between the armpit and elbow and ask the question. Upon them answering they are to push down against the two fingers you have holding up against their arm, with all their strength and you will clearly see that if the response is the truth; they have all the strength in the world to push down against the force of your two stationary fingers. If it is a lie they will not be able to force your fingers down and they will have a sliver of the strength they had on an honest answer. This is because while you might lie – the body will not lie for you. It refuses. The tell-tale signs are subconscious and out of our control. The most visible giveaway is when a person is lying and they answer the question as to whether they are or not – they might say 'no but their head will be nodding 'yes' whether they know it or not. A perfect example of this is watching Michael Peterson 'nodding yes' to the question as to whether he killed his executive wife. He himself should watch the replay of this so he can try to keep his head still in subsequent interviews. Pay attention to clips you see on TV about someone who has been found guilty of a crime they are denying. It's shamefully and ridiculously obvious. As stated, TV advertising is the best avenue of seeing deception in action. The only time the head nodding 'No' gesture is used in truth, is when the party is in Disbelief.

The fastest way to find out if you have an optimist or pessimist on your hands in work or your partner is to give them a pen, ask them to put it in their mouth and draw a circle on a piece of paper. The action of how they hold the pen is the cue. If a person holds the pen with their teeth in a subconscious smile, that is the mark of a positive mindset person. If the pen is held by the lips you will see the subconscious, frowning action that comes from it. This will be indicative of how this person sees and addresses life in general. Whether to the positive or the negative.

A lying person's emotions don't fit what's being said – look for the quick expressions of emotions. This is something that requires ongoing practise to master but once done so, you will readily see in micro expressions, what a person is truly feeling, regardless of the words that leave their mouth. Anxiety and fear leaks in deception. It becomes easier to spot as you look for it repetitively.

More importantly for you, a life of deception, in any form, is indeed a harder road to travel. Having won a poetry contest in the US; the poem published, was called "SIN" and a simplistic explanation of the road ahead is noted in a few of the lines:

"Toss & turn while you sleep
Think. Think. What to say next…
Just one word, now is text"

Referring to a Yes or No answer. Self-explanatory one would think. If you don't answer honestly a lie, like Pinocchio, grows and grows until it's as plain as the nose on your face. The Pinocchio Effect is when the blood vessels in your nose contract which makes you want to scratch it. People with good game don't use that game to lie and cheat their way through life – they don't need to. Allow yourself the peace of mind an honest life brings. Be an example to others, be the person others aspire to be like.

It's when we cheat, lie and steal, living an 'incorrect life'; that the conscious mind tortures us by making us lay awake at night, paranoid of the little things and 'occurrences', that the person living a wholesome life just simply does not have to concern themselves with. If you live a 'sinful' life (so to speak) and you are not mentally tortured by your actions, there is a high probability that indeed you are a psychopath. They are the only ones without a conscience, without empathy, they are glib and remorseless. I'm not saying you haven't had a brain injury to your left frontal cortex or amygdala, which is causing you to be void of the sensitivity and emotion... just that you have a tendency void in those who feel and care.

Attraction: Dilated pupils / fluttering eyelashes / touching of the arm / body points toward the attracted / eyebrow raise or flash when first see / lips part / feet point towards the party interested by.
In love people laugh too much / look too happy about nothing / have fixated eyes / irregularly high heart rhythm.

Eye contact longer than normal (than in passing). Eye contact can be made as much as 40 metres away, we know and can sense someone looking at us across a crowded room (secret glances as opposed to piercing or blank stare look - we can still feel those) / Eyes widen and pupils dilate / Hold direct eye contact for longer intervals (than you would with a colleague for example). Habitual liars often know that eye contact is a sign of truthfulness and will maintain this contact for the purpose of deception / Head tilting, active listening / May mirror. If your target looks from your eyes to your mouth and then back up to the eyes, this is one of the most positive signs of attraction / Run their hands through their hair / Touch the arm as part of conversation. Look out for the micro eyebrow raise when meeting someone new – they like what they've seen. If anyone smiles with still eyebrows, this is not a genuine smile.

To Be Attractive: Make yourself scarce after the first few dates / Never give the impression you are sitting around waiting / Ask good questions whereby you can incorporate "Me Too" / Listen attentively / Mirror / Open body language and stance / Stand tall / Eye contact / Smile / Don't answer emails and texts before twenty minutes expires otherwise you'll look like you are sitting by the phone. Men don't like to linger on the phone so get your organising out the way, a little chit chat and then excuse yourself saying: "I have to go; I was just heading out the door." Notice the full stop there – Leave it at that... not adding "cos my psychiatrist doesn't like me being late" or that you have something as mundane as a haircut appointment to get to. Leave some element of mystery / Always return missed calls within 24 hours (socially and business) / Disclose low risk, deep details about yourself and measure that you are getting reciprocated self-disclosure / Be yourself – it's what you're best at. Be light-hearted and interesting "I'm a really bad dancer but that doesn't discourage me in the slightest"/ Move to medium risk disclosure after the first few dates (hopes-dreams-ambition-family). For a woman accept a date no later than Wednesday for Saturday. If you accept a date on Friday for Saturday you will subconsciously give off the cue that you are sitting around and possibly that you don't have enough of a life of your own / Don't blab about your insecurities and weirdo-ness on the first date / Never talk about an ex unless asked directly and then no need to tell your date that you wanted to set your ex's car on fire for revenge or go into any detail. "Yeah he was not for me, we had different goals". People will often disclose the worse things about themselves on a first date. Listen – do not disregard the red flags (i.e. my ex thinks I'm obsessive-compulsive when it comes to cleaning) they are telling you that they had some difficulty in this area (i.e. I flip out if you so much as leave a coffee cup on the table) Listen and Pay Attention genuinely. Know a smile without eyebrow movement is fake and a smile whereby the lower jaw is dropped, is one that has been rehearsed perhaps in front of a mirror. Additionally, a smile with the upper and lower teeth showing is forced. One needn't or mightn't go as far as excessive couch jumping per se when they feel attracted. That may be perceived as over-action in an attempt to convince; for example. I mean this in the broadest sense and not in the manner worth suing for.

"Let yourself fall in love. If you haven't done so already you are wasting your life. DH Lawrence

Anger: First and foremost on the point of anger – Anger is about Control. Anyone exhibiting anger towards you is attempting to control what you think, feel, behave or all three depending on the nature of the anger. Angry people will often hold their breath in speech, attempting to stifle the anger from being released at the level they really feel. Tight lips with a puffing is indicative that this person really wants to cut loose on you and maybe it is society itself, that has already noted their anger maybe out of control or inappropriate. I'm not certain if it is just coincidence or it is so, I have had many working experiences with

people who displayed both inward and outward anger with the commonality of Dark Blue eyes. Naturally there's the aptly called Black Eyes experienced from murderers and people without a 'soul', the thousand mile stare, or a brown so dark it appears black but this ongoing coincidence of Dark Blue eyes is certainly worth a mention as they have somewhat of an explosive demeanour (in criminals anyway). It is an anger that erupts without any sense that they are able to control themselves and what they do next.
Jutting or pushing of the bottom jaw forward / Clenched jaw / Crossed arms with fists clenched / Finger pointing – when a finger is pointing in a gun cocked motion, it is an intentional display of anger.

The Psychotic Mind: What's this doing here you may ask? People with game should be able to see an unbalanced person from a mile away.
No pain threshold / extremely low reaction to what the average person would find repulsive / No conscience / More often from an abusive background (although one would think; if you knew firsthand how bad something felt, you would think twice about doing it to another person; but that is the very nature of psychotics – they do not care). A history of animal cruelty / Left Frontal Cortex or Amygdala damage from an injury or accident / Sometimes a previous Peeping Tom or panty pinching charge / Arson.
The saying "it's the quiet ones you have to watch out for" most certainly was originated by people who

were referring to psychopaths - they disclose the least and not because they intentionally do it but it is the absence of feeling that makes them the best at deceiving.

A psychotic's brain injury can be exposed with some simple reaction techniques – one of which is the inability for them to follow one's finger from side to side. The disconnection denotes a brain injury and in grasping their hands, sliding your hands down from the base of their palm to the fingers – a person with this mindset cannot help but grasp your fingers as they slide off – even when they are told not to move their hands. Some pictures of serial offenders, serious ones, show they have notably small thumbs – I read a thesis on it, yet I'm still not certain how that is. Needless to say, if you spend any time on handwriting analysis you will see that even the briefest signature gives an enormous level of insight to a person's personality. The enlarged capital letter = high self-esteem/self-approval. The slant of the writing to the front = someone who lives in and for the future, as a backward slant denotes a person who has not let go of the past and the things that hold them there; as does an unslanted straight handwriting denotes someone living in the present/now. The list goes on and depending on what level of communication skill you aim to achieve, you will have to spend a great deal of time reading up these subjects in a detailed format.

In a sales arena: As the seller, you absolutely do not want any of the following hand or facial movements from your buyer:

Face turned away facing downwards – you have not gained their trust – they do not believe a word you're saying.

Tilting of the head for a period longer than 30 seconds – they are not interested, they are bored, as too with the obvious head resting in hand looking downwards motion. Yet a quick tilt of the head shows interest. The time element differentiates the two.

Indecision is shown by a pulling of the earlobe – you have not effectively sold the benefits of your product and why they should go with you over another company of the same nature. Backtrack to where you lost them. If you don't know where that was, revert to the probing questions: "If you could change one thing about your business in relation to (_____) – What would that be?... Our company offers that service/has longevity (whatever they said they'd change)".

Arms crossed – they are blocking you out (check temperature of the room not causing it). Hand them a piece of paper to unlock this stance.
Eye rubbing is a sign that they do not believe you (check they are not tired/upset or have an irritated

eye) – all or most of these positions can be undone by handing them a piece of paper.

Closed eyes – denotes a negative thought pattern is occurring regarding your pitch.

Pinching the nose bridge is showing impatience and also denotes a negative train of thought that they are subconsciously or consciously moving towards.

If they rub their hands they have done research.

Touching the neck – they don't believe you.

Importantly: Nor do you want their feet facing the door as they are subconsciously making a run for it. Apprehension is shown by locking of the ankles. People who think they are controlling their body language often forget about the feet – they are your greatest barometer to measure how you are doing. If they are sitting with crossed legs kicking the foot – they are bored. You require the open relaxed stance of open legs (no not that open). To unlock a foot stance hand them/slide a piece of paper across the desk but make them reach forward to get it. It is harder and uncomfortable to keep one's legs crossed when leaning forward. Make use of this for a quick fix.

When they stroke their chin they are deciding. Ask them to buy your product and shut-up. Don't say another word until they have spoken. He who speaks first loses. The silence can be as deafening as it may be long; shut it and keep it shut till they speak. If you speak first, after asking them to buy, you will lose the sale. Oftentimes, when you practise this technique you will find i.e. they ask another question (you haven't dealt with all objections clearly) or outright say "ok". If they ask another buying question all is not lost, clarify and ask them again "do you think this product/service is right for you?" If they say yes don't hesitate to go straight to the part of "how will you choose to authorise it – MasterCard, Visa (your company's options) etc..."

However I will say; as the Buyer – Never tilt your head for more than a full second. If you don't like the price offered cross your arms, any salesman trained will know he's losing you... smile quickly and then stop if he's trying to win you back with another, more reasonable offer. And if you can afford to let the item/service go; if this doesn't work – get up and walk away. It will make sure he is offering you the lowest price possible if you go back.

I am available for training sessions to "Get Your Game Up" and these topics will be covered in greater detail in the Sales Master sessions. If intense and thorough detail was used in this doctrine, I fear I may bore the living daylights out of you. Especially if sales is not your chosen field. This book includes the basics of what you need to know to have Game.

The main aspect of the Sales series of sessions teaches one how to be A Closer. The Game series is more on the Social Interaction side.

Now to the other important aspects of Body Language messages -

Dress: Is imperative to making a good impression. Period. People judge you by how you appear so dress yourself accordingly to the circumstance. Whilst language is the yardstick by which your intelligence is measured, outward appearance is the equivalent of how you are first perceived. If you prefer to go barefoot – save this for camping or a day at the beach. It is abhorrent to see someone in the shopping centre barefoot, what do you think we're in your living room? If you require office attire, dress for success. Navy, black, grey and brown, known as the power colours, are the perfect suit or office attire colours. As dull as they may be, they show you to be a sound and sensible individual, willing to be a team player, as most often people will use these colours. Bright pink is not the colour of the day in the office. If you have a flair for colour – splash it with a scarf or other soft accessory, do not make it the main item such as a blouse, shirt or definitely not your pant (Slap). If you are meeting the person you are dating's parent/s for the first time, these same rules apply." If in doubt – go without" should be your mantra regarding dress code. Sensible is the best appearance for most non casual functions. Casually: jeans with a pair of boots and a dress shirt for the men. If you tuck a shirt in you must wear a belt with anything with belt hooks. If you don't wear a belt you may as well wear no pants at all, for the impression it makes. My one friend went through a whole job interview and when it ended, the CEO said to him that "if he wanted to make a good impression" he mentioned "he should have put his belt through all the belt hooks". Needless to say, he didn't get that job. You only need to make a mistake like that once without being on the hyper-alert about it in the future. Look one last time in the mirror, give yourself the once over before you leave for anything important. Ladies: in the summertime a simple sundress with a heeled shoe, high enough to extend the calve muscle. Always wear pantyhose in the office with a skirt. Dress according to the weather. For example: a buff guy wearing a t-shirt when it's freezing cold outside is giving the impression he is a show off, more so than his musculature would in the summertime. And for the love of god, any god, wear deodorant and do not let your body odour be the thing a person remembers most about you. It's unnecessary in this day and age when there's a convenience store on every corner. There's no excuse for body odour. Do you hear me - None.

Colour: Something worth a mention when discussing body language is the language of colour. There are power colours and colours that soothe and colours that make you tense without trying.
There is a jail in the US that has all the prisoners wearing light pink. Even the underwear is pink and

the tough nut Warden of the prison is glad to say, to anyone who asks, he has had no incidents of violence in his prison. Personally, I think contributing too is that it could be that they're stuck out in the middle of the desert and it's too dang hot to fight and get all hot under the collar, but really it is to a certain degree, the effect the colour pink has on the psyche. Soft pink, not the blazing bright shades of pink. So here's a rundown on the colours and what effects/impressions they have on the human condition and its influence on behaviour and moods.

Black – West symbol of mourning – East rebirth / Formal / Concealing / Slimming / Dark / Mysterious/ Elegant.

White – Purity, Innocence / Virgin-like / In East used in mourning (careful) / Sterile / Bland effect / Creates space (painted room)/ Wholesome / Kind / Angelic.

Red – (Warm) Extroverts favourite colour / The warmest colour / can result in anger when room painted / Fiery / Bold / Courage / Dynamic / Confident / Intense / Strong emotion – Anger (seeing red) / Love / Warmth / Comforting / Don't wear to important engagement / Action / Chinese Good Fortune and Prosperity / Red dress = Sex Appeal.

Pink – (Warm) (light pink not loud pink) Soothing / Quiet / Unable to act aggressively – non threatening / Contented / Peacemaker / Calm (Macho males don't wear the colour pink because of the subliminal soft message it gives off).

Orange – (Warm) Enthusiastic / Attention Gaining / Intense / Power / Associated with the sun.

Yellow – (Warm) Anxious / Stimulates nerves / Uplifting / Attention Seeking colour / Anger if room painted / Frustrating / Used heavily in advertising – traffic signs / Draws the eye / Creative energy - yellow notepads.

Brown – (Warm) Conventionality / Practical / Reliability / Orderly / Dull / Strength / Stable / Down to Earth / Labourers / Depressed feeling (painted room) / Unnoticeable / Indifferent.

Beige – (Warm) Run of the mill / Conventional / Blend in / Earthy tones / Good colour to splash with louder colour.

Blue – (Cool) Calm, Relaxed / Sincere / Serenity / Depressed mood (feeling blue) / Dark Blue Conservative when worn / Painted room in workplace is excellent choice / Colour most often worn by men.

Grey – (Cool) Efficient / Stable / Neutral / Detachment / Unimaginative / good colour to splash a louder colour with.

Purple – (Cool) Spirituality / Royalty / Imaginative.

Indigo – (Cool) Calm / Intuitive.

Green – (Cool) Calm / Order / Tranquillity / Harmony / Balanced / Jealousy (green with envy) / Wimbledon players sit in the Green Room as relieves stress and has a calming quality. It is now painted another colour but still named that – subconscious. Many firms use Green Rooms.

Full Moon Behaviours: Police Officers, Nurses and anyone in the health care field will tell you quite candidly, there are noticeable changes in the public and people on nights when the moon is full. While not a lot of study has been done on this topic (comparatively), there is evidence brought forth by very reputable people that there is indeed a physical change brought to us by the monthly cycle of the moon. In England in the 18th century one could make a plea of "Lunacy" (derived from the word Lunar) and if he murdered at the time of the full moon he would get a reduced sentence. A new moon also brings very troubling times in the criminal arena, for example the Menendez boys killed their parents on a night of the new moon. Statistical studies clearly show the murder rate rising with the full moon and falling in the first and last quarters of the moon cycle. It is said whatever frame of mind you start out in on the night of a full moon will be enhanced and exacerbated by the fullness of the moon. If you are feeling down you will feel markedly more depressed about whatever is troubling you and if your spirits are high - they will soar. People's behaviour is definitely more erratic at this time. It is said, it is because the human body consists of approximately 80% water and this relates directly to the effect the moon has on the tides.

Finally, at the risk of losing any credibility I may have gained thus far, I must at this time address astrology. Not the read in the paper, one twelfth of the world will have this happen to them today type of astrology. More so, the astrological personality traits which decipher (albeit in a roundabout way) how a person is more likely to behave, how they will perceive things and other intimate things one can't tell via another aspect. Mentalists, profilers and other such professions will often refer to this in their fields; just because it can be so blatantly obvious what a person's star sign is based just on their behaviour and mannerisms, or for example, the way they dress. My take on it is that people don't hand down an art form for thousands of years if it has proved in its entirety to be false and there's no truth to it. Vedic Astrology is practised in India and the Far East and still to this day for an arranged marriage to go ahead; the charts must align in harmony for the marriage to proceed – it is one of the things that can get a person out of an arranged marriage, if their charts do not align.

So it's the behavioural traits of these signs that assist you in being able to read the people who fall under them. I've been trying to force myself in a less forthright (or nicer) sign than Leo and try as I may –

the personality traits of the other signs do not suit me. Try it yourself if you are reading on in disbelief. Moon signs are also prominent indicators of how a person may behave. These two signs can be pinpointed (per person) by the day, year and time of birth which will advise where the sun and moon were at the time you were born – hence, the sun (external – what one shows the outside world) and moon (internal – what one does not show externally) sign for each person. Unless they were born as next door neighbours in this world, at the exact same time chances are these signs will be very individual, as each person is. Employers can see what traits they want in their new hires, what they have on their hands and how a person is most likely to react to adversity, change or pressure for example. And how to maximise their staff based on appealing to what makes them tick. Remembering you are at liberty, and in fact I expect you would, go on to do your own verification, of the things written about in this book.

Since I'm treading this fine line for the intellectually inclined or towards conservatism; I shall go on to say: Psychic ability is something one can learn much like learning Japanese or any language – of course there are some people who are natural linguists, picking up something so foreign quickly, and others to which the study of a language is a longer road, involving many years of devoted study. This ability is much the same. Doreen Virtue and Sylvia Brown are world renowned psychics, making appearances on CNN, Larry King Live and other conservative, intellect based and non-conservative programmes. They both will readily tell anyone who asks, that this is indeed the case. Doreen Virtue also does training classes with impressive results from believers and non-believers alike. Research it. It has long since been known that the police forces around the world enlist the aid of psychics. There is so much more to this world that we cannot see, feel, touch and make into tangible objects or processing. Statistics show we use 5% of our conscious brain on a daily basis. What then of the other 95% and our so named 'Junk DNA'.

There are things that we aren't aware that we see, and subconsciously we are not aware that they influence our decisions.

CHAPTER 3   TALK LANGUAGE

It's not what you say – it's the way you say it.
                                                            USA

No sweeter sound to a stranger or friend alike, than their name. It subconsciously places one in the realm of knowing that person, on an intimate level enough to both know and use their name.

Talking involves much more than just words. There's Pitch and Projection, Volume and Timbre of the voice, and of course, the Emphasis we strike on certain words to make a point. Like Body Language, most anything one reads on Talk Language will address very much the same things.

We all have verbal altercations with strangers - my last one, years ago, ended in me whispering: "Don't make me break your spine in front of your children" before it escalated to the point of no return. Because of my body language and confidence she did not doubt for a second I could or would (not that I really would) – she went back to her seat on the bus. You can train yourself to bluff that. It's not what you say, it's how you say it and you can say anything you want if you can control your voice.

TONE: The tone of one's voice is the most readily ascertainable as to whether the person speaking is, for example light hearted in their message or is ready to bite your head off. The tone, unofficial though it is, is imperative to get aligned to the message you want to send if what's said is to be received correctly. The Pace of what's being said is too, as it is an effective way to add urgency. If there is a fire and you're calling 000 Emergency – you wouldn't talk in a slow, methodical manner, although perhaps one should so the message is made clear the first time. Yet more so, the message is in a higher pitch than is normal for the caller, also with a faster pace. You would find Emphasis on words, syllables or sentences, in this instance.

When someone speaks slowly and with notable time gaps when answering a question – they are most often being deceptive. Then in the exception of, the natural occurrences, whereby a person is commanding in the regular course of conversation, another to listen to their every syllable with boringly long gaps; this only makes for people wanting to finish your sentences to hurry you along. If you find that people are often offering up the last word of your sentences – you may very well fall into this class of talking. Speed things up and see if things change.

The Volume of the voice has a high variation level subconsciously and consciously. When one talks for longer periods of time it is more noticeable. Volume varies from a whisper to yelling. Ever had a conversation whereby you/someone says: "Shhh keep your voice down" one person is talking loudly and the recipient is whispering in an attempt to control the volume. 'Shhh-ing' a person will most often make them talk louder; especially if it is in an argumentative nature - but if the conversation is kept up with the other person all but whispering, without them shhh-ing, subconsciously the other person will speak softer and softer until they are both speaking with much the same volume. Have you ever tried yelling while someone is whispering or speaking softly to you – you feel like a nut; hence the body and voice moves towards equality. This strategy works well in telephone sales when the operator is sometimes yelled at, like they themselves did the damage and are not the messenger.

The Pitch of the voice also varies by what's being said. Some people have a melodic pitch and their voice could be described as Sing-Songy. That bugs the human ears; so if you have an overly melodic pitch to you – that requires work. The voice of deception leaks when it rises higher on the untrue words of the sentence/s.

An example of Controlled Pitch, Volume, Projection and Pace, is when tennis players Maria Sharapova, Victoria Azarenka, Serena Williams and a few others these days; do that high pitched squeal of theirs when hitting each ball. These noises are not imperative to them being able to hit the ball, they are voluntarily, controlled and matters of choice rather than a requirement to being able to play well. They are much different from the grunt of exhaustion often heard in a 4 or 5 set men's game. From a physiotherapist's perspective – yelling of any type will actually increase the strength of force put behind it. It's not like a weightlifter can increase his performance by 50% or anything that much better. Allegedly, it would be lucky to change the effect as much as even 5-10%. The men tennis players rarely if ever do it and they still win matches. How many times do you hear Roger Federer ever grunting up a storm – a man wholly in control of his voice (and most everything else it appears). His ongoing silence is the concern as one never can readily tell what's going on in his mind. The same can be said for female tennis player Agneszika Radwanska. I sat through the 2011 Australian Open Tennis Final of Sharapova and Azarenka – heavens; what a sound extravaganza that was.

Another good example of voice control is when you hear advertising, compare the sound of the voice of the Whatever-O-Matic guy to the lullaby sound and softness of a funeral company advertisement. Quite different versions of overall Volume, Pitch and Projection. Decide what voice you need and use it appropriately when required. For Example: One wouldn't use their library voice for a presentation in a crowded room, as such – nor vice versa, bellowing in a library.

Timbre is the sound of a person's voice which changes in quality. If you sang like a rock star for a night, the following day, the timbre and volume of your voice would be hoarse.

When people have a sore throat they whisper, however, it takes more effort from the vocals cords to whisper than to speak at level volume; so in essence they are doing themselves no favour.

In a Sales Arena: You would be amazed at how unwittingly and frequently a salesperson can shoot themselves in the foot just by what has come out of their mouth. Self-Sabotage is most prevalent in the love and public arena areas. This is where you can combine your new found Body Language knowledge to test if you have gotten into the sub-conscious of your mark, and visually see if you are influencing them effectively. See (read) what they are thinking by how you communicate.

There are two types of Questions one can ask:
Closed or Binary – These questions elicit only a Yes or No Response. In sales they are to be asked only when the response is a foregone conclusion of Yes; as you wish the person to begin the Yes-Mode of Behaviour. If you ask a verbal list of questions that illicit a No response, chances are, when you get to the part where you ask them to buy your product they'll still be thinking subconsciously no, even if they made an enquiry and called you to come there. Getting a person out of a No-Mentality is both time consuming and exhausting at best. So you will begin and end

with the Yes-Mentality. An example of the Closed Question would be:
"You like your money to work for you, instead of just sitting in an account doing nothing right?"

"Do you want to save money in this aspect of your business?"

You'd have to be a fool to say No, so the forgone conclusion is these questions will get the Yes Response. Forcing a 'yes response' works in a familial or social setting too.

Open or Non Binary – These questions are good in the investigative part of the conversation where you are learning about your customer and their needs. None of these questions can be answered with a Yes or No (without sounding like a kook) Think of the Five Steps of Open Questioning = Who, What, When, Where and How.

"When was the last time your (whatever field) needs were reviewed?"

"How do you know you're gaining the most advantage if you haven't had a look at it in ___ years/months. There have been many changes in our industry/company... over the last (years/months) – it will only take twenty minutes for me to review it with you and make sure your gaining... yak..yak..yak.

Most anyone can spare twenty minutes even on a lunch break – you say one hour (+) and you're toast, it has a different psychological impact.

Nobody should be asked to 'sign' a contract – just 'authorise'. It is far less stressful. People don't like hearing that they 'spend' or 'buy' – women 'shop' and men 'invest'.

There's stock standard sentences and questions that can be asked to make sure you are talking to the person who does the 'authorising,' not the stand in man who can't put pen to cheque. You have to qualify the person, make sure you are talking to Mr or Ms Right; this can be established as early as in the greeting. Set a series of Trial Closes (gets them in Yes-Mode) and then go in for the Real Close question/s. Up—Selling is always an area most forgotten about, as too is Referral. These assist in longevity and must not be overlooked, as any good sales manual should stipulate. Words and phrases add to your level of persuasion. Communication is powerful in the sales arena, and should always be with the intent to have an outcome; even if it is that you are talking to the decision maker.

In An Argument: Firstly, the recipe for winning or not acting like a child, in an argument Cool, Calm & Collected is the way. COOL, CALM & COLLECTED. It'll never change. If you cannot get involved in a heated discussion in this manner; opt out till you can put your point of view over in an adult-like manner.

Screaming, shouting and throwing things are a sign you have not yet matured, and this can be especially dangerous in the workplace. Don't do it. Do Not.

Secondly, one should never embark on a topic of discussion, in which you are not well versed. You are better off saying 'I have to read up on (the topic) before I can contribute to this discussion' than to have made the appearance that you are talking out your a$$. You will save yourself the impression that you talk for the sake of talking, and don't know what you are talking about. When you opt out saying you need to read up on a topic; you appear to have sound judgement even in the preliminaries of an argument. Histrionics and hysteria are best saved for those who will readily forgive you or not hold it against you albeit; they may quietly think you're a nutter, i.e. your partner, or members of your immediate family (yet even they don't deserve to witness you out of control).

Life is about control or the perception you are in control. When you cut loose in a heated encounter you almost instantly lose. The main thing in an argument is that you remember to breathe. Taking a deep breath replenishes the oxygen to your brain and makes you more alert, and more likely to recall correctly words spoken which can be reversed back to make your point.

In an argument take the course of action whereby you deliver the hardest point to combat first.

For example: At a dinner, a heated version of whether the Americans really landed on the moon when they said they did in the 60's occurred. They had gone through the part where there was a flag waving with no wind, no stars visible from the surface of the moon, no blast crater visible from the landing, astronauts footprints visible but the 17 ton landing module makes no impression, no visible flame from the rocket and so on…

The conversation got heavier and heavier, until one person asked a man to my left what his thoughts were on the matter, since he 'had not yet commented'. He stated almost matter of factly: 'not to encourage the conspiracy theorists; yet they have brought up a few very interesting points, one being that the craft would have had to go through the Van Allen Radiation Belt which is 6 miles deep. However, they were the only astronauts not to have experienced the sometimes severe, radiation burns of all the space missions up until now. Ordinarily the Van Allen Belt would incinerate anything within the first two miles but they came through completely unscathed; at a time where interspace travel was in its infancy, I mean, they are still having fatalities to this day, yet such a complex mission was completed successfully in 1969...however, more interesting is that television uses AM signal for the video signal combined with FM for the audio, 30-300 mhz and 300-900 mhz. So claims that television signals from the moon were broadcast on the lower 500khz bandwidth; which is AM only – well that certainly makes for more query'.

Everyone shut up. No one had the answer or anything that would come remotely close to an explanation, so they all sat there dumbfounded. Their initial impression was that he had no knowledge of this particular topic, and that's why he sat it out. All the heat went out of the air and we went on to more socially mild topics, such as the Unsinkable Titanic, and her two sister ships, the Britannic and Olympic which also sunk.

Note; no question was asked or left open at the end. He didn't say "so what do you think of that?" or "how do you explain that?" This point of view showed clearly, there were many questions about this landing that have been left unanswered or are unanswerable. It is all but futile to continue this topic on with this being the case.

So therein lay the most controversial and hardest to combat point in that argument, there is nowhere further to go. That is an example of the best strategy for winning or silencing an argument-to-be. When one indulges the trivial points of no consequence, an argument can form and finish with no resolve or end. It then runs the danger of the same conversation being picked up at a later date and carried on. Make a strong, effective point calmly and you will leave everyone with the impression that they best not take you on. In an argument there is sudden stress. Force yourself to breathe out so the body is then forced to need a deep breath in, gushing oxygen to the brain when clarity is most required. Make a conscious effort not to hold your breath under and in any circumstances – now that you are aware of it, watch how much you do it.

Guilt Reversal: Is a common stimulator of arguments. For example; when a husband is cheating (hypothetically speaking) he may, in an argument, accuse the wife of cheating when she is plainly not – this is known as Guilt Reversal. He is attempting to put blame and guilt on the wife's behaviour when it is he in the wrong. Oftentimes, when you are in an argument and you know definitively that you are not in the wrong, yet the other party is getting ridiculously upset; that is most often a clear attempt at Guilt Reversal. It is easier to say: "Hey I'm not in the wrong here so stop trying to make me out to be the guilty one". Let that be your first and final statement, so it will be less likely for this person to attempt guilt reversal on you again. It is the Human Condition not to consistently repeat things we have found unsuccessful previously (except in love and who can explain that).

With the uncomfortable silences that occur in conversation – don't overtalk to fill them. Let them pass, as they do. That ends up being a sign of deep friendship when one can sit with another and the moments of silence are a measure of comfort and familiarity.

Argue with the composure and precision of an athlete or refrain – do one or the other. Breathe.

In relation to talking one must discuss Listening. Listening is a hard skill to master and people go late into their years being unable to listen effectively. As the old adage goes – we are given 2 ears and one mouth, so use that as the ratio of how much talking one should do, in relation to listening in a conversation. Listening involves not butting in, if you interrupt a person speaking, not only do they lose their train of thought, but also at the end of a conversation, they will feel as if they have not been heard. Someone whom we shall refer to as Butty-But-In, and recall the day her young son said: "but Mum you never listen". So if it makes an impact on one so young, you can imagine how an adult feels if this is one of your habits. Easy to see what her New Year Resolution should have been, it was that she practises the art of listening. She butt in three times while having that conversation and continues to do so to this day; it is a very tough habit to break. She justifies it with 'yeah I have a bad habit of that" you said it sista. If you know you have a habit others have called you on – work on getting a handle on it. It must be noticeable if someone has picked you up on it. Butt-ers are the people, (aside from the people who talk nonstop) others describe as '...You can never get a word in edgeways'.

Effective listening can be faked by something so simple as shutting your mouth until the person has finished speaking, nodding and making the 'hmm' sound at important points and reiterating and repeating back what they have just said in the guise of: "just so I understand what you're saying clearly, you want..." at least this way the person will Think you've been listening even if you have not. If you absolutely must interrupt do so by saying "let me just stop you on that one point/ May I please just interrupt you for a moment regarding..." at least that way you will be taking ownership of your poor listening skills. If you butt in because you don't want to forget your point you can always go back to it on "what was that point about ____ you made?" It most often will refresh your memory on what you thought at that time. Think of a key descriptive word or put a mental picture of an object, animal etc. for recall enhancement.

Reminder: (because of how important it is) One can't speak and hear at the same time. Interrupting when someone is speaking is a no go zone. If you have something relevant to add and interruption is necessary, state: "Just quickly on that point". This can be used in sales for an objection raised which you have something to add that can minimise the objections' importance.

In some professions such as Sales and Psychology – you will be out of a job if you can't listen well and master that skill effectively.

Additionally, in regards to Talk Language you can look for which eye of a person's two is more open than the other. One will always have a notably more open eye, as this indicates whether the person is a right brained thinker or left. Right represents the Creative nature and Left represents the Analytical nature. But the brain's hemispheres work on the opposite side so be aware of this. You can align and tailor your conversation to which side the person most relates to.

CHAPTER 4   ETIQUETTE

The World is like a book, if you don't travel you don't get past the first page
                                            Israel

Etiquette on a whole covers, for the most part, the varying aspect of manners and education towards acceptable behaviours in public. While there are no degrees of honesty – Etiquette does have degrees and broadly depends on how you were brought up first and foremost, more often, what took place in the family home. If it is acceptable for one to talk with their mouth full and eat with their mouth open at home; one would be hard pressed to learn on the outside that this very same behaviour is predominantly thought of as vulgar and offensive. It is, and it is not till someone tells you that you pay attention enough to see others don't do it. Eating is a subconscious behaviour which, outside illness, one can do as a function without thought. It is not something someone who does not know any better will think to look and improve on. The degrees vary in that some will think, depending on increased social status, that not having knowledge of wines is ignorant and why ever would one select a smooth white to have with a thick T-Bone steak. So here are some tips on the basics of etiquette and manners – enough to get you through a fancyish dinner without appearing inexperienced.

First things first – an overly successful American salesman once told me "To get through life and be able to sell to anyone; you must first learn at least five minutes of every subject you can think of a conversation coming up about – and "<u>march to the beat of their drum.</u>" I learnt about golf, football, knitting, cars, boats, camels – you name it. It is suggested in this book that you do the same. It gives off an air of being versatile and more so, interesting. And that is after being well rehearsed with the up to the minute news and current affairs of the day. It is ever so pleasant for anyone to meet people who share their interests, a shared commonality if even only for five minutes. It is very easy to change topics either to a similar subject or one completely unrelated after approximately 5 minutes. This leaves someone with the impression that you know enough about their interests to appeal to them. Subconsciously they will warm to you as their brain has triggered the thought – 'he likes what I like'. Having always thought the game of cricket is perhaps the longest, drawn out, most boring game in the cosmos for a great many years; yet knowing all too well there are many folk who are deeply passionate about this sport – I can talk about it, doesn't mean I have to like it. No-one I have ever spoken to about cricket would ever believe that is my opinion while the topic is being discussed. Simply watching the sports portion of the news can give you enough ground to discuss the outcome and shortfalls of a particular game – I'm not saying one needs to be a Rhodes Scholar about it. There are many shortcuts, figure them out and use them. This works for dating as well – find a person's interests and read up on them, so you are able to seemingly share their interests and likes – whether you do or do not.

This concept is not about manipulation or falsehood– it is about strategy and commonality. Would you want to buy a product from or date a person similar to you; or someone you didn't have the slightest thing in common with? The Human Condition shows we choose 'like over opposite'. Opposites may attract initially, especially in the dating sequence, however if a choice is presented, 'like attracts like' in the end. It's the way of the world.

Manners & Class: Class is a visual. This is most readily seen when you watch someone on television or the movies, someone who exudes class or can be described as 'elegant'– in their dress, poise, and manner. But then they do an interview and open their mouth to speak and you're like "who the hey is that?" A quick voice lesson would stop that impression but oftentimes people don't see in themselves what others see. Additionally, people think they know about the very things they don't know about.

Wines: Names & type of wine = Grapes Name. Example = Cabernet is from the Cabernet Grape/Chardonnay from the white Chardonnay Grape. This is really easy – Light (white) wines go with Fish and Chicken dishes. Heavy wines (red) with Meat dishes. The lighter the wine – the lighter it looks – Chablis, Sauvignon, Pinot Gregio (lightest colour and flavour) Chardonnay has a heavy colour and oaky flavour, it is the heaviest 'bodied' white wine. Red the same – in order of heaviness: Pinot Noir, Merlot, Cabernet Sauvignon and Chianti last and heaviest. The lighter reds (not past Merlot) can be had with fish and chicken as some people only drink red wine. Same as a heavy Chardonnay can be had with a meat dish. Read up on first and feel free to mention the light fruity flavour of the (white) wine (read the bottle as it's being poured so you don't get the name wrong). Reds are described as having heavy peppery overtones (Cabernets) etc.

"What's your favourite grape?" I once asked my snooty wine-aficionado-in-her–own-mind friend and it really stopped her short. For the average wine drinker does not know that the grapes themselves cause the name of the wine. Whether the Chardonnay grape, the Merlot or Cabernet dark, red grapes ... and so the list goes on. You've seen red and white grapes at the supermarket – think of it like that and expand your knowledge from there. When you have selected the wine at a restaurant – you will be shown the bottle to confirm it is the correct selection and be poured the same to taste it. Take a small sip, swill it in your mouth (silently) and comment: "Outstanding" is a good word to play it safe. See how your dinner companion/s treats the wait staff to see how they really are.

If you are the host of a dinner party - Serve food from the left side and remove plates from the right side (least intrusive) – this will make your behaviour uniform to the finest restaurants in the world. If you are at one of those dinner parties that have numerous forks, knives and spoons – the soup will always be served first and to keep it simple; know that one moves from the outside in. So the teaspoon is last for coffee/tea, soup spoon first and when you move outside to in you will naturally follow suit of what is the expected course and according utensils. Your bread plate (and cutlery when casual) is always the one to your left. The fork is to be held points down and food put on top with a knife – fork not to be used in a shovel motion unless opting not to use a knife on a casual brunch or dinner occasion. One should use a knife when set. Knife and fork to be placed parallel to each other in the middle of the plate when the course is complete, and the dirty plate is required to be removed (this is a sign that the dish is completed. If the knife and fork are in any other manner – be prepared to be asked if you're finished prior to the dish being removed). Ideal compliment = "That was outstanding" – don't use repetition. Think of other descriptive words if the same was used with the wine. "My compliments to the chef" to be said only at completion of entire meal. Don't leave the table first or last. If declining dessert say something light hearted like "I don't deserve it".

Don't laugh overly loud. Keep your elbows off the table. Don't talk with your mouth full. Think fast –

speak slowly. Be Quick-witted – Ladies: master 'quiet allure' (or at least the impression of the quiet giggle at the appropriate time/ a small smile etc.)Keep your legs together parallel when standing, crossed at the ankle when sitting – this way, nothing you do will be offensive to even the most stuck up guest. Having learnt your 5 minutes of each subject you can ever remember having had to hear or speak about – you should be good to go. Remember it is not a sin to say you'll 'have to read up on (subject) before contributing to this conversation'. People will respect you for your honesty.

In General: No Spitting / No Swearing / No Gossiping or Saying Bad Things about people (it says more of who you are, than it ever will the person you speak lowly of).

Speak in a calm, assertive tone (shows confidence) with neither high emotion nor pitch. If something is exciting – that's different. No Shouting, Screaming, Wolf-Whistling to anything nor behaving as if you were brought up without discipline. Be silent when in doubt. Act Reserved (even if you are not) – Don't air your dirty laundry. Keep your skeletons in the closet; no-one needs to know your past. Your past remains in the past, if you do not repeat the mistakes made, and learn the lessons that were given the first time. If you have made a mistake, admit it to the relative party, apologise to them and bystanders and move on. Don't bring it up again. Be humble about your achievements and status in life. Braggarts are seen as empty and void of depth and meaning, not to mention boring to be around.

CHAPTER 5   SOCIAL INTERACTION

You never get a second chance to make a first impression

USA

I am going to endeavour to spend my life with the mindset of my favourite German Shepherd, Quinn. He was the nicest soul inside that body which let him down to arthritis. I got an angry little Chihuahua, an outright beetchy Shitzu beetch, and Poppy who I rescued out of a plastic bag in a trash can in Karratha; needless to say she had a plethora of problems by the time she came to me. Additionally, I had two cats who thought it was funny to swat Quinn in the face with claws extended. He took it all in stride and nurtured each one as they grew with the patience of a parent – he judged no beast even Poppy with her half mouth. He did on the other hand judge every man with testes – he just wasn't into tall or big men. But that mental attitude he lived with, appeared to me that every action he indulged in only came from a place of love, and the purest love that we often see in a loyal pet, especially dogs. He never forgot I rescued him and he was always there to rescue me (at least in his mind). When the vet came to put him down I was happy to let him go having just learnt the extent of the pain he was in and loving him so much I couldn't bear to see it. That was the fastest recuperation from any loss. Where there is birth there is death – where there is love there is grief. He lived a full rich life and stayed as long as he could. It was incredible to see the animals gather around him as his body lay on the mattress awaiting pick up. They looked sad and acted sad (including the cats) in that no one had an appetite for at least two days, they saw him the night before and how sick he was and they reacted in a way few of us credit animals with. The day of thinking animals don't have feelings, with the documentaries on chimps and other great apes and dolphins, show us what was really subconsciously known all along - animals have feelings just like all living things. Treat them accordingly. When people are overwhelmed with regret (over natural cause) that maybe they didn't do the entire right thing by that person or creature, they experience a deep sense of loss. Maybe knowing the time for making it up has now passed. My dog lived an indulgent life where he was much loved and that certainly wasn't the road I found him on. It is with this thought and belief that life is a cycle and that death is but one destination on the journey, where we meet again, and if life requires – are born again to fulfil the lessons we have not yet mastered. We stay together always. Always.

A Beautiful Mistake (Sanskrit) - My Quinn

I'm not going to outright say: be as kind as a dog is, but subliminally, that's what that previous rhetoric was about. In doing so, people around you will come to have the same heartfelt fondness of you for your kind and forgiving nature. Point.

If you have a phobia or fear that affects you or your ability to socially interact – try Exposure Therapy. It works; you will feel free and liberated and it quells your other insecurities stemming from the phobia. When you defeat the thing that scares you the most, you become well aware that there is little else you cannot accomplish, if you put your mind to it. I remember the guy asking me how I felt in the plane I was skydiving out of to alleviate my fear of heights. I was so scared, wanting to vomit and could envision vomiting all over myself falling out of the sky. I told him "I'm beyond freaked out right now". When it was first suggested my response was: Hell No! But there I was up in the sky with no soft place to land. Apart from the fact I thought my heart would stop and screaming till hoarse, I didn't die as I suspected I would and now can say - The thoughts no longer control my life. This measure will attend the same to you. There are professionals to assist you if you can't do it yourself. Whether your fear is warranted or not – it needs addressing for you to live a full life. Start your plan on it today if this relates to you.

Full Moon Syndrome & Interacting– ask any medical professional or police officer if they don't believe people play up when the moon is full. In actuality, when people are out of control, the staff themselves will say "it must be a full moon out". Given the body consists of predominantly water, it comes as no surprise, like the rise and fall of the tides; that we too wax and wane with the moon. Mostly if you are already feeling in high spirits, the full moon will exaggerate this euphoria. If you are feeling depressed at this time, expect to feel it even more so when socially interacting this can be a good time to sit it out or if you are feeling like it – go out at your own risk to anything of huge importance to you. If something is scheduled at this time of the month (no not that time but yes that time too come to think of it) Don't Drink Alcohol – it will quadruple your chances of an adverse behavioural reaction if you drink too much.

KEEP YOUR SECRETS SECRET: Keep Your Secrets to yourself. It is the only way to guarantee your secret will be kept silent. There is a saying in America: "The only way three people can keep a secret is if two of them are dead". If someone asks you to disclose the contents of a secret – ask them: "Can you keep a secret?" if they say 'yes' – say "so can I" and leave it at that. You have been entrusted with information of which someone truly believes you will be responsible, loyal and not tell. You owe it to them to show your loyalty is true. This of course is not in the event the secret kept is one of harm – they hurt someone physically, stole, raped or murdered someone etc. that level, anything that so much as borders on the illegal. Then it is your place and duty to this world to tell the proper authorities. An FBI agent had to report his own son, after he disclosed to him he had intentionally killed a couple in a car. As admiral as his behaviour was – he also protected future people being hurt and changing the course of others' lives. He stopped a potential domino effect.

How many of us can say our loyalty to the community at large runs that deep? Weigh up this possibility, if someone is stupid enough to blab to you about this level of misgiving, you owe it to society to do the right thing regardless.

The Jailhouse Confession has led to incarcerating future criminals as they wait for their trial – locked up in that close proximity with other 'like-minded individuals' – it is easy to let one's guard down. Remember, whatever your circumstances – people who are trusted, are to have earned it over a period of time or are not trusted at all. People with game don't blab endlessly nor do they waste speech on gossip. The amount of times people have given a jailhouse confession whilst awaiting trial; and that same person gets set as a witness against them, is incalculable. And still they do not learn – 'there is no honour among thieves.' Much less murderers and rapists. Criminals by and large, are notorious for not keeping their mouths shut - which leads inevitably to their own demise. One job I did was to extract information from various notorious criminals, and then filter it on to my superiors. They made it so ridiculously easy for me to do that job.

KEEP YOUR SECRETS SECRET.

TIME: Time is short you hear everyone say – it's not that life is short, except for some, as the average lifespan is 85 years old and that will only increase with technology – life extension is inevitable so you must make good choices and be happy with your actions in this world. If you live till 70 you only have 25,550 days; make the most of them. Plan for your future – make sure you make a nest egg for your retirement and know that life is not at all that short but you will be wishing it was, if you go into your post working years with no money or not enough. Prepare. Time is short with some people – those who have had someone die from cancer, lost a child, had any kind of major tragedy befall them with another, will tell you the time you spend with people is short when you don't necessarily want it to be...and that's the "time is short" people refer to" – the stuff that regrets are made of.

Regret only the things you didn't do – not the things you did. Learn to say, when within reason – Yes, instead of the instant No that may be habitually your response. Step outside of the comfort zone and/or the walls you build around yourself for protection. When you step outside the walls, you may get hurt, but behind the wall there is still pain. That is why we must make the most of our time and cherish - let it be known to our loved ones while it's happening. Your sentiment is worth nothing when the relationship is over, irrelevant to how it was lost.

I have dealt with other aspects of social interaction previously and these also pertain here without having to repeat them. The obvious of interactions hold true – be kind, don't steal, lie or cheat, the Ten Commandments (or at least the last five of them) are a good guideline even if you are not religious. They have stood the test of time for well-being and conscience free behaviour which is a necessity for people with game. I shall mention them in order in the event you are not familiar with them. It matters not from where they came, the last five can be universally met – they set a good moral standard: 1. Honour thy Father and thy Mother 2. You shall Not Murder 3. You shall Not Commit Adultery 4. You shall Not Bear False Witness against thy neighbour 5. You shall Not Covet thy Neighbour's house, nor wife nor anything that is your neighbours. The first five relate to religion so I'll leave them out. Anyone of that faith knows what they are, and those not of that faith will not be offended or think it doesn't pertain to them. The words are not cite specific and 'thy neighbour' could be your workplace or those around you in general. Don't want something of someone else's so much so that you steal it or harm to obtain it in any other suspect way. Bearing false witness encourages one not to be a rumourmonger or the like – don't say bad things about people. If someone is bad he/she will have their own cross to bear – leave them to it and you just worry about yourself. Given enough rope any wrongdoer will hang themselves in their own way and time. Nerr you worry.

I am entering notations in this doctrine about serial killers, psychopaths and sociopaths as it's a part of having game - to be able to protect yourself and see them coming. This makes for easy recognition of whom and what you need protection from. Whether it is by a self-defence course at the local council or whatever is available to you depending on how much you want to spare your life in the event of...

Even in the notorious case of Ted Bundy – nobody who knew him would have dreamed he was capable of such things. These dangerous psychopaths are effective just by their ability to be normal in every way: functioning job, family and every social aspect. Yet the dark side of them exists, the secret side, as much a part of them as the rest. You have to trust your gut if it tells you something is up with a person, your own radar will have the hair stand up on the back of your neck, if you go to a house that is filled with morbid and depraved items of an outwardly 'normal' person. If you have not had the chance to learn self-defence I offer this advice: If you are in a bad predicament - "GO FOR THE EYES" with all your strength and with the intent that it may be the last thing you do. Don't do some half-hearted, feeble attempt 'in case you might hurt them' – If you get your fingers into the top of a person's eyeballs, pulling downwards and dig into them as hard as you can while pushing their chin up with the base of your palm. It's agonising but that is your best chance of immobilising the perpetrator and preventing further harm coming to you. I wonder what law I've broken in advising this. I'm sure to hear about it. The self-defence course I trained in through work taught me, amongst other things, how to stop a person's heart with one blow (a martial art manoeuvre called 'the one inch punch'), how to get out of a headlock, and what to do if someone attacks me at an ATM machine... you don't have to be that enthusiastic, but take the best course you can afford which offers you the most protection, relative to your world's needs and requirements.

Gut Feeling & Intuition are your own silent assets. Follow what your heart tells you and you will follow the path most suited to your future. The body itself tells you when 'something just didn't feel right' or 'the hair on the back of my neck stood up'. These are the body's way of saying 'No don't go into the forest at night alone – someone might be out there waiting to harm you'. Harm or otherwise, be aware of your body's attempts to guide you in the right direction, you can't always rely on noticing the double eye-blink of a pathological personality. The more you are in tune with what your gut feels - the more readily it will be read. If you are put in a situation of having to choose; rely on the voice inside your head that tells you what it is. Hopefully at this late stage of this doctrine – you have calmed the negative messages you tell yourself and now only accept positive feedback from your previous insecurities. That negative voice must be silenced with a commitment to not adhere to any of these messages – the 'I can't do that' rhetoric should only be applicable if it refers to a deceptive action. I want to/will rob a bank because I have no money – the voice that tells you 'no – don't, you can't do that, you'll end up in jail' is indeed your intuition telling you the probable outcome of your intended action. This is the difference between the intuitive voice and the negative voice. The area where intuition requires your utmost attention is when it comes to deciphering another person, or their intentions. I stress the importance of this as a matter of course, as it can change the outcome of your future if you trust the wrong person. There are predators in this world, more than you would care to think of, or ever believe certainly, yet all together too often, people fall prey to their charms and graces.

Beware of the Controlling personality. The controlling personality knows neither limits nor boundaries. They care of but one thing – themselves and their own desires and well-being. Controlling is usually first noticed when they ask one not to see their friends anymore. This then extends to the absence of family members; thereby rhetoric of belittling occurs to where the person abused sees no self-worth; and believes the controller is the only one who wants them. If the threat to leave the controller occurs, threats from the controller of harm to the person, or their family member/s will soon follow for the most part. A person exhibiting controlling behaviour is not showing any aspect of love – they are showing their ability to be unbalanced. Escalation is something that is readily noticeable to the abused parties. This is the Relationship Psychopath. A relationship borne of countless arguments and intense making up sessions is commonly misunderstood to be acts of passion and love. This is not at all the case; and this type of relationship is one destined to fail on a monumental scale.

The Industrial Psychopath is the workplace person who, for example, may pretend not to know who the boss is and then coincidently finds themselves talking to the said person. They may, by incident, have chats with the boss whereby other staff see and are left with the impression he/she is 'in with the boss' or 'in the know'. Or ingratiate themselves to people who are actually close to the boss, and tell them stories of their achievements, or the non-achievements of other staff, especially the person whose job they want. They are glib, oftentimes popular yet are devoid of any empathy which can be noticed in their behaviour over time.

To explain in essence how a predator thinks: Tommy Sells, a convicted serial killer described it as such – "I go to bed and I dream about it, I wake up and I think about it – it becomes your drug." He openly states: "I hated the person who did all that junk to me, and then I became the person I hate" he says of his early emotional trauma. He was also diagnosed with schizophrenia. This behaviour goes beyond habitual into the obsessive. But not one person could tell just by looking at him that this was the case.

Serial killers and people with an especially violent streak do not look like sadistic psychopaths... but then again, what does a person that sick look like? That is often the reason they get away with it so long

– they look and act normal. It's their 'averageness' that makes them often invisible. They have no capacity to empathise and as such don't care for the feelings of their victims. Studies show they literally have blood that runs cold – their brain scans don't register distaste to pictures of violence and death the way it does for the common and balanced person. They really, just don't care. It has been proven that people's perception of pain decreases after having being 'rejected', it is rejection, abuse or perhaps a brain injury or a combination of these factors that makes for the future psychopath. Know that these are the traits and circumstances. Murderers are born from people you'd never expect. These people are dangerous when met at any level. Be aware that they are out there, in multiples more than you think, whether it is the anti-social personality, psychopath, the Industrial psychopath (active in the workplace) or the weirdo across the hall from your apartment you might feel sorry for. Many an innocent stalker relationship has been borne from this level of deception. When criminals get a sentence of 'life in prison' for a crime so punishable; I wish Longevity to them. I'm hoping there's a special place in hell for these types of criminals.

Cleckley's List of the Anti-Social Personality is as follows:
- Superficial Charm
- Above Average Intelligence

- Absence of Anxiety and other Neurotic Symptoms – has considerable amount of Poise, Calm and Verbal facility
- Disregards Obligation / No Sense of Responsibility
- Untruthfulness / Insincerity
- Antisocial Behaviour / Impulsiveness
- Poor Judgement / Failure to Learn from Experience
- Pathological Egocentricity / Total Self Centeredness (inability to form lasting relationships – real love or attachment/no deep lasting emotions)
- Lack of Insight / Inability to see self as others do
- Ingratitude for special considerations, kindness and trust
- Objectionable Behaviour (Vulgarity / Rudeness / Quick Mood Shifts)
- No history of genuine Suicide Attempts
- Impersonal, Trivial and Poorly Integrated Sex Life
- Failure to have a Life Plan or Live in an Ordered Way

Furthermore, he summarises: "...More often than not, the typical psychopath will seem particularly agreeable and make a distinctly positive impression when he is first encountered. Alert and friendly in his attitude, he is easy to talk with and seems to have a good many genuine interests. There is nothing at all odd or queer about him, and in every respect he tends to embody the concept of a well-adjusted, happy person. Nor does he, on the other hand, seem to be artificially exerting himself like one who is covering up or who wants to sell you a bill of goods. He would seldom be confused with the professional backslapper or someone who is trying to ingratiate himself for a concealed purpose. Signs of affectation or excessive affability are not characteristic. He looks like the real thing."

Hare has a Psychopathy Checklist which is detailed in the following order:

1. GLIB and SUPERFICIAL CHARM - the tendency to be smooth, engaging, charming, slick, and verbally facile. Psychopathic charm is not in the least shy, self-conscious, or afraid to say anything. A psychopath never gets tongue-tied. They have freed themselves from the social conventions about taking turns in talking, for example.

2. GRANDIOSE SELF-WORTH - a grossly inflated view of one's abilities and self-worth, self-assured, opinionated, cocky, a braggart. Psychopaths are arrogant people who believe they are superior human beings.

3. NEED FOR STIMULATION or PRONENESS TO BOREDOM - an excessive need for novel, thrilling, and exciting stimulation; taking chances and doing things that are risky. Psychopaths often have a low self-discipline in carrying tasks through to completion because they get bored easily. They fail to work at the same job for any length of time, for example, or to finish tasks that they consider dull or routine.

4. PATHOLOGICAL LYING - can be moderate or high; in moderate form, they will be shrewd, crafty, cunning, sly, and clever; in extreme form, they will be deceptive, deceitful, underhanded, unscrupulous, manipulative, and dishonest.

5. CONNING AND MANIPULATIVENESS - the use of deceit and deception to cheat, con, or defraud others for personal gain; distinguished from Item #4 in the degree to which exploitation and callous ruthlessness is present, as reflected in a lack of concern for the feelings and suffering of one's victims.

6. LACK OF REMORSE OR GUILT - a lack of feelings or concern for the losses, pain, and suffering of victims; a tendency to be unconcerned, dispassionate, cold-hearted, and not empathic. This item is usually demonstrated by a disdain for one's victims.

7. SHALLOW AFFECT - emotional poverty or a limited range or depth of feelings; interpersonal coldness in spite of signs of open gregariousness.

8. CALLOUSNESS and LACK OF EMPATHY - a lack of feelings toward people in general; cold, contemptuous, inconsiderate, and tactless.

9. PARASITIC LIFESTYLE - an intentional, manipulative, selfish, and exploitative financial dependence on others as reflected in a lack of motivation, low self-discipline, and inability to begin or complete responsibilities.

10. POOR BEHAVIOURAL CONTROLS - expressions of irritability, annoyance, impatience, threats, aggression, and verbal abuse; inadequate control of anger and temper; acting hastily.

11. PROMISCUOUS SEXUAL BEHAVIOR - a variety of brief, superficial relations, numerous affairs, and an indiscriminate selection of sexual partners; the maintenance of several relationships at the same time; a history of attempts to sexually coerce others into sexual activity or taking great pride at discussing sexual exploits or conquests.

12. EARLY BEHAVIOUR PROBLEMS - a variety of behaviours prior to age 13, including lying, theft, cheating, vandalism, bullying, sexual activity, fire-setting, glue-sniffing, alcohol use, and running away from home.

13. LACK OF REALISTIC, LONG-TERM GOALS - an inability or persistent failure to develop and execute

long-term plans and goals; a nomadic existence, aimless, lacking direction in life.

14. IMPULSIVITY - the occurrence of behaviours that are unpremeditated and lack reflection or planning; inability to resist temptation, frustrations, and urges; a lack of deliberation without considering the consequences; foolhardy, rash, unpredictable, erratic, and reckless.

15. IRRESPONSIBILITY - repeated failure to fulfil or honour obligations and commitments; such as not paying bills, defaulting on loans, performing sloppy work, being absent or late to work, and failing to honour contractual agreements.

16. FAILURE TO ACCEPT RESPONSIBILITY FOR OWN ACTIONS - a failure to accept responsibility for one's actions reflected in low conscientiousness, an absence of dutifulness, antagonistic manipulation, denial of responsibility, and an effort to manipulate others through this denial.

17. MANY SHORT-TERM MARITAL RELATION-SHIPS - a lack of commitment to a long-term relationship reflected in inconsistent, undependable, and unreliable commitments in life, including marital.

18. JUVENILE DELINQUENCY - behaviour problems between the ages of 13-18; mostly behaviours that are crimes or clearly involve aspects of antago-

nism, exploitation, aggression, manipulation, or a callous, ruthless tough-mindedness.

19. REVOCATION OF CONDITION RELEASE - a revocation of probation or other conditional release due to technical violations, such as carelessness, low deliberation, or failing to appear.

20. CRIMINAL VERSATILITY - a diversity of types of criminal offenses, regardless if the person has been arrested or convicted for them; taking great pride at getting away with crimes.

Seldom is it the case that people score 40 out of 40.

There is untold controversy about Capital Punishment and the Death Penalty which asks if there is anything more archaic and uncalled for. Given the overtones of this book, you may be surprised to find that I'll put forth the argument For the death penalty; even though I'm not supposed to (we're not meant to be perfect, we're meant to be whole). I cannot force myself to (after working within the criminal justice system) think that some people do not deserve to die for their actions. Having heard first hand in court and seen myself of crimes so horrific, so cruel; and the criminal making a plea agreement, to get a lesser charge and in some American states, save themselves from going to trial and risk receiving the death penalty. The death penalty should be reserved for people, who have committed crimes so atrocious – that they deserve to die for their actions. Why shouldn't someone be made to pay with their life, for violently and brutally taking another person's life? When you have someone who is, well, behaving like a criminal because that's what criminals do, and then asks the court for mercy for themselves, when their victims have the right to remain 6ft under, you can see where the conundrum lies. It has long since been noted by scholars and criminalists alike; that people who offend on this high scale activity are not able to be rehabilitated. There is zero to no chance of that change ever taking place within them. In very serious crimes and behaviours – the die is cast. They will just reoffend if they are ever let out of prison. While life in prison is quite punishing in and of itself, these severe offenders do not sit there thinking about the crimes that put them in a state of imprisonment – they have no conscience, they do not care. So why would remorse be a factor for consideration. Oftentimes they can be seen to parrot the verbal intricacies of regret; yet they have a shallow and hollow tone to their voice and have no facial motions which typify deep regret. Whereas you or I may have an emotional breakdown from having murdered another person; to them it has the same meaning as passing the salt and pepper or opening the refrigerator door. These people can be readily noticed and the red flags noting them as such should not be disregarded. Your intuition will be the first and foremost telling sign. Some people outwardly just feel 'creepy' or 'make your skin crawl'. If the hair stands up on the back of your neck - Listen. Like pain telling you that the body needs to stop, so too, does the body tell you when to go.

Handwriting analysis of a person with a disjointed mind usually shows as a certain disjointed scrawl on the page. This analysis is dependant also on the size of the lettering, pressure of the pen and multiple other contributing factors. Like body language analysis – always seek 'pattern clusters' to confirm your impressions are correct. Otherwise surely we'd all be thinking our doctors are as nutty as a fruitcake.

Learn Self Defence and First Aid – you never know when you will need either. People who have children absolutely should have at least one parent versed in First Aid, though herein it is recommended for both parents to have that training. Your child's life may depend on it one day. Emergencies of any nature are time sensitive. Be Prepared. Circumstance may not offer you a second chance.

Inner knowledge of knowing these two assets will give an aura of confidence about you that all the money in the world cannot buy. When people act like a jacka$$ around you, almost looked bored by their behaviour. Your body language will not show fear and you will not look like a suitable target. Clint Eastwood them. One never sees him in a high pitched frantic panic. Cool, Calm and Collected is the way to go with this knowledge, in the case of threat or emergency. Breathe – it will help you be most effective with your approach.

In the car driving when you want to say "get a move on you demented fool" – Refrain. A stressed driver poses the exact same threat as does a drowsy one. Endeavour to make driving a thing of enjoyment, an unexpected break in your day, make a traffic jam your opportunity to have a break. When you want to cuss at a traffic jam - know there could quite possibly be a fatal accident ahead causing the jam; and there are people who have no idea their life is about to change in a way they never dreamed possible.

CHAPTER 6   DATING/LOVE

Lust alone cannot sustenance make
Australia

Some of you will have rushed forward to this section when you haven't found the haystack much less the needle in it; to pick apart all the tools you could possibly use from here in relation to your own situation. Well then especially for you - I'll start here. Don't skim, you'll get to the good stuff – relationships on their whole are about Patience.

Firstly, an action made from love never hurts anybody; in your quest to harm no-one nor then can there be serious ramifications in anything you do. I'm talking about the genuine love from your heart and not the jealous, possessive love we have all felt from time to time or in our immaturity.

Ask yourself if any behaviour you know you are doing is not conducive to your well-being: Are you habitually attracted to the wrong person for you, give more than you take, are you always the chaser instead of the chased? True love and the person who truly loves you, will have the element of reciprocity in it. They will give you back as much as they get. Not in a monetary sense but in an emotional barter. You will not feel used, verbally abused or whatever it is you see as the shortcoming in your relationships time and again. Speaking of which, a person who loves you would/should never call you names or say bad things that hurt you – that is the nature of someone trying to control you. Love is about someone who lifts you up and supports you in your chosen path – not someone who tries to stop you in any way, shape or form. True love is a coming together of equals, mutuality, you should not want for if the person you're with is the One. If it is the One for Right Now, well that's just a waste of time really. Some people would rather have something over nothing – but if that something causes you misery (in any form) what is it worth having. Start a new cycle of dating only people who respect you, your thoughts, goals and anything else that is important to your future health and well-being. If a person does not enhance your life, and detracts from it – exclude them from your selection criteria being met. A life partner is a positive enhancement on the life you are already living and nothing less.

Have you found love or have you found what you have chosen to settle for? Have you found in another person your addiction, a dramatic toxin. Have you found the things that make your parents appeased. What have you found for yourself - Are you happy?

Ask: Is this making me happy or is it time to move forward and change it? 'Advice is something we ask for when we already know the answer and wish we didn't' someone once told me. You owe it to yourself to do the right thing For You, for a change.

As best you can, remove yourself from alcohol induced poor judgement – there's a starting point. Within reason, buy what you want. You deserve it. Treat yourself to anything and any amount you would spend on a lover – Love yourself at the minimum amount you would love another. You would defend a loved one when wronged – why not defend yourself and your own beliefs and wants in life. Chances are you are at your kindest and most considerate to the people you love, give that gift to yourself. Be kind in your choices that involve you and what you want, you'd do that same thing for someone you love wouldn't you? 'Settling' is for those who accept second best. If you settle for second best you can guarantee that's exactly what you'll get; your happiness and future will be compromised. Hold out for the real thing whether it's your job, a relationship, your passionate hobby or any other aspect that fills your world. "No" is not a dirty word. People will martyr themselves for what others expect from them. Learn to divorce yourself from the things others want for you and replace that with what you know will make you happy. People who have good game have prioritised their wants, over what others want for them and are coming from an inner place of harmony and connectedness.

It really is important you divorce yourself from the things other people want for you - A bad marriage is one of the worst things one could do to themselves. It's not enough that your parents or social circle will live happily ever after, from the choice you made for their approval – it's about what makes you happy.

Additionally, you have to know the whole package you're getting and you can't tell that just by considering the wrapping. A leopard can't change its spots – it is what it is. To think that marriage or having a baby can change a person or circumstances is unrealistic. Either you are happy with the person you've chosen or you are not – expecting someone 'to change for you' will only lead to further disillusion and disappointment. Be realistic with who and what you have on your hands and decide if you can accept the baggage that comes with.

When one door closes, another opens; but we often look so long and so regretfully upon the closed door that we do not see the one which has opened for us.
Alexander Graham Bell

Now to the really important part – You. Yes you. Would you like to date you? No joke. Think about it... would you want to date you under the present circumstances – do you act the way you yourself would find unacceptable? Do you come up short? Well then, you'll have no trouble finding out the root of this cause and that part of your circumstances you adhere to today, may be of your own making. There was a time that I thought I would not like to date me; so I took the time out to get whole and happy within myself so I might actually be the person I wanted for me, a person I could stand to be around for long periods of time – and be that person to someone else. Some people just don't get that you have to be whole yourself to have a healthy & whole relationship.

Do you replay the behaviours of the past expecting a different result? Taking 'Baggage' from past relationships into your new one is so 90's. Get the bleep over it and move on – how dare you blame someone who, for the most part, you hadn't even met when all of that happened. That's a cop out and a poor excuse for attention seeking behaviour – stop it if you are doing it. Think about how ridiculous the whole concept of that is, no less so unhealthy. Anger of some kind usually follows along with that behaviour...and please don't be mistaken – Anger is an attempt at control. People usually carry on angrily when they have lost or are losing control. Guilt Reversal being the perfect indicator of this. The cheating husband angrily accusing his wife of an affair. Old Hat.

If you think you might have screwed up a relationship you wanted – chances are you did. If there is nothing you can do to save it (in reality not in Stalker-Land) then you have no option but to let it go and chose not to exercise those behaviours again – so you at least give yourself a chance of not having that same series of events play out. There are few things so unattractive than being over someone who keeps hounding you...and still being pursued by a person after you have moved on from them. This decision is in the best interest of you and in reading this book you have started the Year of You; and this unhealthiness should be the first thing to go.

Take it for the lesson it is, learn not to do those same behaviours – let go & move on. You have no choice you know – It invokes feelings of pity, ridicule & if it continues, disgust. Get out of there while they still have that nagging thought about whether they did the right thing. Release that person to get on with their life lessons. Hate and anger are most toxic to you, while the other party goes on their merry way.

Above all else – know when to say 'When'. Obsessive desire, it is said, is a monster that falls on its own horn. The condition is terminal and will meet its end, whether sooner or later – its fate is sealed from day one.

Try going on a first date to something with a little excitement to it. Something that makes the heart race faster than it normally would. Recalling how couples – especially those on a first date came out of a Circ Du Soleil show – they were downright giddy as the circus itself electrified their senses. That was after all Circ's main mission and an easy way to trigger feelings of exciting love. Don't give your feelings up too early into dating or a relationship – You might scare people. When you know someone likes you, you like them more. Stop. Assess. You will feel emptier if you date someone just to have someone. Eliminate that as an option.

While forbidden fruit tastes better - Cheating is so ridiculous; if you want to be with someone else go and be with that person, instead of dragging your partner down with false hope and unrealistic plans; made around a person that isn't even being honest with them. No really, get going on your way. If you ever loved that person do them this favour. Let them get on with it, the pain of your loss won't kill them – they'll get on without you. Your leaving will be the best thing that happened to them they'll see in hindsight. If your lover chooses to spill the beans about an affair they had and for your own lack of confidence, you take them back – know that you will be playing the same role again one day whether you find out the next times or not. What you allow a person to get away with – they will do again. It's human nature. Why not, they got away with it the first time. And if you are the recipient – 'what they do for you they do to you'. Nothing will make you exempt from that possibility, after all you have witnessed firsthand what they are capable of. Nevertheless, a broken heart is a better and bigger heart.

Be alert to when someone's actions don't match their verbal sayings and cues. For example; your guy saying he came directly from work, but is wearing evening attire, all black, aftershaved up. Unless he aspires to be Disco-Johnny in the workplace, something is amiss. These things scream out at you when you know what to look for. Above all else listen to the voice in your head which gives you the gut feeling – that all is not right. Trust it. Believe it will do the right thing for you, to protect you from harm. If you are in a relationship with someone who hasn't ended with the last person completely or similar circumstances; don't sook if you find one day that you too, have been cheated on. Come to expect that this is indeed a very real probability for outcome. A watched pot eventually boils.

When having met someone new and at the early stage, one can't be sure how long the road will be, but presently you will feel all the trappings of love. The giddiness, the palpitating rush when this person is near but remind yourself to 'be cool'. Don't give too much away in the early days – chill and let things naturally run their course. If he's off with his friends for a night on the town, play it cool and there's a better chance he'll wish he was there with you. Instead of giving the royal grilling say: "Have a good time – mind how you go". Promise yourself if this one is important, to take everything you ever learnt from past relationships and apply it here; so at least you know if it falls apart at the seams - it won't be because of something you did wrong in the past and repeated, only to learn the lesson for the second time (if not the fifth). I also encourage reading up all one can about the horoscope of the person you want to attract/be compatible personally or in business with. Additionally, there are both sun & moon signs of a person – The Sun being what they present to the Outside world and the Moon being their true Internal stance. That's not to say that in the daily newspaper that really will happen to one twelfth of the world's populous – but the characteristics of each sign is pertinent to the person's behavioural course. Chinese Horoscope signs are also beneficial to know – they really hit the nail on the head with the characteristics and behaviours of each animal and its representative. The first warning sign will be laid out in black and white.

Again, I'm not saying the things you read in the newspaper on a daily reading are accurate about each star sign, because that would mean it would have to apply to approximately one twelfth of the world's population on any given day – what is historically believed though, is that the basic qualities remain the same of that person and the time in which they were born. Now just keep your head about you and this relationship will have as good a chance as any. Previous words of advice stream to me – "Treat them like it's a blind date your mother set you up on" Supposedly and especially with women to do to men, it makes them come a runnin'. Being in love is hard work, giddy 24 hours a day, one track mind, that complete loss of control but that does not take away from it being one of the most enriching experiences one will ever know. Parenthood, I am told, supersedes this.

If you are scared of love remember the theory of Schrodinger's cat, a paradox from the Austrian physicist: there is a cat in a box with a vile of poison – no one knows when the poison will be released or if it already has been and the cat is dead. The cat might be alive or dead based on this random event. No one can possibly know until the box is open, whether the outcome is good or bad – one has to open the box to find out which it is. You have to try or you'll never know. Schrodinger's Cat has more to do with quantum mechanics than love but it can be shown for the paradox that it is, regarding possibilities and probabilities; there are no scientific answers to questions.

A kiss can change your future. Most prostitutes will do everything but kiss. There was an incident whereby a security guard for a large money delivery company, had an employee who was an integral part of a large robbery heist. When he was caught he was asked about the girl who influenced him into it, if she was incredible in bed or something. He said he 'only kissed her once'. If you don't like the way a prospective partner kisses, chances are you won't continue on to a relationship. But if you do; it can bring upon you the most intense sensations relating to love, whether warranted or not. The memory of it can generate an illusion of being something better, than it may have actually been. Giving a kiss is not something one should do willy-nilly. Much less the rest of it. If you 'put out' too fast as a woman, a man might be inclined to think, and rightly so, that you gave it up all too easily to however many men before him. What they do for you – they do to you. Have respect for yourself and wait an appropriate amount of time so that the allure and mystery has a chance to grow.

When you know what's at the finish line, one becomes indifferent to the excitement of it all. In the old days they called it courting, which in essence, is just taking the time to get to know someone first without taking all their clothes off. Three months courting period is not unusual. Have enough respect for your body and soul. Your body is the one thing no-one can take away from you without your say so (not including rape of course). Circumstances can make it such that they can take away your house, your car, your money, yet no-one can take your body and self-respect away from you without your consent. Know that this giving of yourself is indeed a large act. Act accordingly.

Life's Golden Rule: Be Cool – about everything in life – Just be cool about it. Everyone wants to hang out with the cool person, I'm not saying Arthur Fonzarelli cool, just the person that doesn't react much less over-react to anything. Make yourself into the person you want to be with. When the serious kind of damage is done it's hardly feasible to go back. In life you train people how to treat you – what you find acceptable, and what your boundaries and limitations are. Visually show you are ok with a breakup and are happy to move on. That person will, at the very least, stop to consider if they have made a mistake and weigh the varying degrees of how big of one they made. The golden rule is to not make any decisions in the first six months, at the end of that time all the facades drop and you see clearly who it is you have on your hands. After the first two years –

you see the raw version of who it is you are dating and then you can make a conscious decision, whether to move forward or get the helluva out of there. Oftentimes it takes nowhere near that length of time.

Sending cards, flowers and all that jazz to someone who has determined they are over you, has the opposite reaction. You might as well approach them in the street and say: "look at what a puss I am". You'll be seen as weak and confirm the doubts they had about you to let you go in the first place. Especially if you are a man: Stalking is presumed by the ex long before you think your constant calling and carry-on is unwelcome. Woman want strong men, someone who shows they can weather a storm but isn't a deeck (Mexican pronunciation) in life. Money, cars and the worldly possessions only matter to a certain type of woman, who label that as their priority. It's who you are when the sun goes down that matters most.

Do you have a gentle soul but a hard outer shell – that's a winner. What appears common in failed relationships is that there is no longer a thread of the person who you started dating. What happened to the fun & interesting guy who used to shower you with attention or thoughtful acts...you want to say: and who are you jacka$$? If you started your relationship on false pretence and pretended to be someone you really weren't, I don't know where you've been living to think that's not going to catch up with you. Historically, a person can't keep up pretence past the first six months. It will catch up and you'll deserve to lose your person for the false advertising aspects of it alone. Shakespeare saying all them years ago – 'to thine own self be true'. That is true to who and what you are, how you feel and express love – Being who you really are will allow the possibility of someone loving you for your real self. And if your real self is an a$$ – well then maybe you need to think about stopping to change those asinine things before you subject it upon the next person you fall for.

Try not to embark on the modern day version of The Spanish Inquisition with anyone under any circumstances.

For the girls – neediness is the killer – some guys like and others avoid the emotional stuff and it is your business to find out which one you have on your hands. Trying to settle the restless guy is a strategy which once again requires you to do the exact opposite of what you've probably being doing all along – If he wants to go out with the boys say: "Sure. I'll make other plans" and then Don't go on to tell him what they are. Be elusive and let him wonder what you do when he's not around – have a full and enriching life of your own and in the early stages of dating; let him know you won't be exclusive until the right guy comes along – that doesn't mean you go out sleeping with other men, just that you accept dates and the company of other men if he's not asking you out. When you give the impression you'll be staying home Saturday night while he goes out elsewhere – you are basically training him into thinking this will be acceptable in the future, when in fact, it is only acceptable on occasion in your mind (and for the imbalanced, not at all acceptable).

Life at its broadest, really does work well with reverse psychology – it works for children and adults who behave like children.

Try it the next time, and if you botched up the last time – get your behaviours right before you waste the next person's time with your antics. Everyone is looking for someone to genuinely love and who will love them with that same commitment in return. Do a version of a relationship autopsy if the demise of one has come prematurely, pick it apart and accept the areas of responsibility that should be held by you and your actions and contribution. Acknowledge your role in the breakdown whether of a friend or relationship, accept if it's something you did which caused the direct demise – adjust your behaviour and move on. Expect a few (dozen) astronomical mistakes into your past. Become the person you want to date and date openly until the one you want comes to the party (so to speak). Dating while you have the hots for someone else can be as simple as going for a cup of coffee with a guy from class/work. It's enough to stop you obsessing about the other one – who, what, when, where and how... when you force yourself to keep shopping around. Even if you know your heart's not in it - you actually gain confidence and self-worth that other guys/girls want to date you and that comes across in your vibe; a strong, controlled vibe of self-confidence and self-worth – now that's attractive. Make eye contact with everyone you find attractive and see what that does for your self-confidence alone. See life as one big opportunity. Keep that in your mindset and don't slouch in your posture and your mind will regroup to accept this mental picture, and the world of opportunity will indeed open up for you, one of which you can only notice when you are paying attention.

And then there's the ex who you thought you would marry only to run into 15, 20 years later and wonder if they spent the time on a diet of hamburgers and toxic waste, that they morphed into this unrecognisable creature standing before you. One must be thankful for those moments. Naturally your first thought when it happens is 'we'd be divorced'.

When all is said and done – the price of love is grief and death is a part of the cycle of life. That is the price you pay for the gift of having a person with you, as a part of your life, for however long the time turns out to be.

Touch: Touch is the most powerful of human actions. A soft and gentle touch on a bereaving person's hand can say without words more than you may ever be able to express effectively or without discomfort. Touch is also powerfully sexually charged. The lightest touch is the most efficient for stimulating hormonal response. Try running your finger as softly, barely touching as you can and see what it does to your sexual partner. Better still run a feather along their bodies going close but not at all touching the genital areas. Touch everywhere but there. Trace around them. Your touch should be as soft as the pressure of the feather – next to none. This same touch can be utilised on a person's forearm in the early stages of a relationship. Touch causes connection. Not too long if you've only just met or just started dating, they might think you're a weirdo. Use the act of touch sparingly and it will be valued. Never touch your boss and certainly not for any period of time, no matter how few nano seconds.

THE BREAK-UP: Spend time outdoors – it's good for you.

If you are devastated about a break up you should take the time to truly assess what went wrong, what part you played and if changes need to be addressed. Otherwise you will continue the cycle of pain & heartbreak and the one you love the most will be another one lost to your quarry of mistakes. You can't expect to be with a beautiful person if you yourself are an a$$ at the best of times. Wonderful people aren't attracted to sour or spoiled personalities, sulkers or mood swingers.

Not many people will disagree that breaking up with someone you love is the worst feeling; that pit of your stomach, dull pain that never goes away and if anything, increases when you see them again. The worst of the worst is when you're not the one who broke it off. I heard it said once: "If you want someone to like you – tell them how much you love them, if you want someone to obsess about you – tell them you can't see them anymore".

I even remember a friend of mine who was about to dump his girlfriend – she dumped him first and he drove himself crazy wanting her back – that's how well that seems to work.

Ever seen the really hot girl with the unattractive guy and wondered what the hey that was all about or – hot guy and Plain Jane – those folks 'got it' because they 'get it'. No-one is ever out of your league unless you convince yourself that is the case. Look to the streets to prove this is true.

If after a break up he/she is not calling you: He has not lost your number, nor has she lost yours. Have you ever got the phone number of a girl/guy you really liked? You tap your pocket/purse all night just to check its safe and you haven't misplaced it already. Know that in The Human Condition 85% of all calls/call-backs or lack thereof, are simply a matter of 'one's choosing'. This leaves 15% to be split between lack of communiqué (as in no phone available) and remote location. If he/she is not calling you back, it's because they don't want to – ok. That's it. That's all there is. You have that person's undivided disinterest.

Love sickness is a chemical reaction which affects our capacity to reason. It lasts at its utmost 7 years, both being in love or broken hearted; mostly at its longest it will take three years before the pain subsides and you are prepared to move on. Security and companionship is what is sought by women. Men look for the child bearing hips and visual traits that show a woman is healthy enough to bear his offspring. Well whoever reading this book hasn't had a broken heart, or is that you have never truly loved another before – that's the only way I can imagine anyone being scar free in this department. This next section is going to be more so about saving face in the breakup than actually getting over it – the getting over it phase has the stock standard practises that are time worn – get out – don't sit at home and mope - distract yourself etc. Time will indeed heal whatever you are going through; it has done it for multitudes of people before you and will do the same for those after you. Just remember you are not the only person in the world this has happened to, and none of them are dead except Romeo and Juliet and they were made up characters. True others have made crude and hasty decisions but had they waited, they would not have made the fatal choices that they did. Just to put things in perspective, remind yourself that as with everything, This Too Shall Pass.

We are attracted to people who look similar to us; we are subconsciously guided by the smell of a person, that also that makes our heart aflutter. The body will be attracted to a partner who you repetitively have sex with even if you are not in love with this partner. The chemicals alter you just by repetition alone.

Try not to feel guilty about your mistakes. No-one can put more shame on you than you put on yourself, for however many years you have done so. Leave them behind you.

The really important part of any break up is that you do not grovel and beg to the person who dumped you – you will only reiterate the very weaknesses and reasons they dumped you for. When you act like your life just barely skipped a beat over the breakup (that crushed you into Jello), you let that other person think you are well rounded, self-supportive and certainly not at home pining away over your newly lost love. It is imperative, especially for a man, not to grovel as this highlights your weaknesses. Be seen out, dating – and that certainly doesn't mean sleeping with, enjoying yourself to the point where any feedback that other person gets, is about how overly effing happy you appear to be. Surely do not talk to their friends about your ex- every word will be relayed back and make you look like the Town Crier.

Saving face through pain is a simple remedy, that becomes important as whoever has done the post break-up grovel is acutely aware of the feelings of shame that get tacked onto your pain. You, under no circumstances want to become the laughing stock of your ex and co. Make them think of you as the one that got away – even if you weren't any of those things when dating (shame on you). You need to have that calm, confident devil-may-care vibe about you, even if you have to fake it – 'fake it till you make it' rings true. You'll do it often enough that your body and mentality will adapt.

If you don't want to make a big deal about something – Don't make a deal about it at all. Take responsibility for your actions once, to the appropriate party, and then let it die without emphasis or review, never make excuses. Most people acknowledge what is an excuse and what is circumstance - unless it is something they may have had neither chance nor inclination to consider, do not mention it. Telling a person you were drunk when you did something and they were at that same party and also drunk – does not rate worth a mention. By the way, drinking and being drunk is never an excuse. Unless you were held down and alcohol poured down your throat. Alcohol-behaviour related actions are entirely the drinkers fault. Having watched many a person try to get away in court, with the excuse of them being drunk/under the influence of drugs – if you have made a conscious decision to drink or partake in drug use; then that is a free choice whereby you are executing and using your free will.

Period. The less you make of a negative situation – the less time it will take to pass.

When to say 'when': Knowing when to give up on love lost, after a stretch of trying with little to no success, is a feat of accuracy within itself. You don't want to pi$$ the person off but you do want to make an impression on their heart. When is When when? When you know in your heart there is no future there and all your efforts from here on in, have been or will be in vain. When you've tried the witty texts without the applicable return in favour, and every other avenue that shows you to be a person-in-their-right-mind things to get your ex back – it's time to throw in the towel, call it a day and move on. For know it is in your destiny to not be with that person as a life partner and that the universal plan has something/someone different in mind for you. Remember the last time you felt this same way and know that it too, did pass, as this will in its own sweet time and place. Someone I knew was devastated by the breakdown of his marriage to an utter beeatch, we did all but blew party whistles when he announced it – now he is with a beautiful woman who just cherishes all the things his ex gave him shiet for. Know that will happen to you too. You will meet the person who is going to be right for you even if you divert off track for a while and get busy with other people. See if you can name one person that you loved – broke up with and never ever got over it nor got another chance at love again. Nah, me neither. You will always get over the devastation of loss (but not necessarily with death) when in a relationship situation. Everyone has before and will continue to do so, after you get over yours. It is human nature to pine loss. But the pinning becomes less and less till you notice you go hours and then whole days without that possession of thought overwhelming your every waking moment. "I'll never meet anyone like her... if anyone knows her the way I did – how can you not love her "will go away with time. The body while it can remember there was pain, is unable to relive it. The brain mechanism clicks off and you can say how much something crushed you or some other descriptive words about how painful it was to go through, but you won't relive that agony regardless of how much you were forced to bear. The feeling itself goes and is forgotten irrelevant to the time memory holds onto it.

Everything passes – Buddhists talk of life just being a circle of events – without life there is no death. Death of something brings space for something new to fill it. It's all part of the parcel. Without endings there would be no beginning – isn't that what they say – the thing about old sayings is they keep getting repeated because they are true. Not because they're a crock that hasn't happened time and again. Say when, move on and give yourself a chance at further happiness. You'll see when you're paying attention, the next person you date is going to make you think 'what the hey was I carrying on like that for.' It inevitably happens that way.

Even though you may find yourself deeply wounded by it – it is still in your best interest to at the least, appear to move on. You're taking away the very thing they took for granted would always be there and it's human nature to want the things one cannot have. If you really like someone and feel them slipping away – try telling them: 'You know what, I don't think this is working, maybe we should see other people'. It's going to work better than begging them to stay. It does take bravery but think; they already had one foot out the door – what have you got to lose besides the nothing you were going to get in the end out of this person anyway.

When you do move on – move on truly and completely, not stifling and ignoring it, as this will just make for some untimely baggage. You owe it to yourself to be treated better, be less abused, whatever. Or if the last person you dated – did nothing wrong, then it's just that you owe it to yourself to give a chance to love. But give love a real chance if you're going to – be truthful to yourself about your limitations and whatever a person might want to know about the person they love. They should know for the most part. And that doesn't mean your experience with the high school water polo team that Saturday night - just the things that will affect whether something in the present is a deal breaker or not. Remember you can only pretend to be or act like someone else for approximately 6 months – and then all your shiet is going to come out in the wash. If you have shiet going on – deal with it fairly and with love. If you have things to fix; maybe take the time out to fix them once and for all, without playing the victim. Then who you represent is who you really are. If you have to hide certain aspects of your nature they need addressing. Fast.

You will inhale Karma if you wish the new person to be a replacement till you have a chance to get back together with your ex. Its plain wrong to do that or to take a new lover in the vain hope of putting the flame out with a fire.

Care deeply and without reserve when you do love – so what if it is not in the cards to last, at least you will have made the most of it while it lasted. They say true 'soul mates are not the people who things are all perfect and rosy with, but the ones who are only with us for a short while and their departure brings us to our knees.' It is the people who we learn the hard and fast lessons with, who cannot stay as it is not part of the lesson, not a reward earned.

Know that life is part of a circle, a cycle and while you thought it was the end of the world last time you broke up with someone – you'll still feel that same way again next time. Know that there's no chance on god's green earth that you're the only one who has had to come out of this situation, and learn every single lesson of your contribution to the failure, so as not to make the same mistakes again. Grow and change; make it your mission to.

Forgiveness is unlocking the door to set someone free and realising you were the prisoner
                                            Max Lucado

Have you been so deeply in love with someone who you've not yet told? It's quite painful and only you can decide if it's worth the risk of disclosing; if the person you feel this for is married, clearly in love with someone else or unavailable in some other measure. Tread carefully; there is karma to be paid on these actions not to mention the chance that your attestations may be rebuffed. I wouldn't want this for anyone; I wouldn't want it for me either. But then again, the most and worst thing anyone can ever say in answer to a question is "No". No one's ever going to take a stick and beat you for asking. That may end a lifelong exercise in futility of "What if..." Having this feeling of what-if must be addressed as the opportunity you let pass or fate deprived you of, whatever the case; and let the indecision of it pass forever. Know that you may never pass the same way again with someone and take the opportunities presented to you as they come. As unrequited or unspoken love in the soul lies buried – silenced. Consider that may very well be the best place for it.

Wealth shouldn't be measured in dollars but in how many people you have in your life who love and care about you. Wealth cannot prevent heartbreak. I read from my friend's aunts correspondence – 'some people are so poor that all they have is money'. The wealthiest people I ever met were some of the saddest people I ever knew. When you work that hard and come home at 9 o'clock at night, you want someone who loves you deeply and truly waiting for you. If you've chosen the trophy wife and she is out with her friends till all hours, at the very least you would have known her capacities when you met her/him.

My one friend drives a Ferrari, has the mansion with the swimming pool – 2.5 kids and a dog... but his wife doesn't love him. She never really did for what I saw. She loved the life he could provide for her and his reward was to be treated as such. Yes she's beautiful, a little bit funny but as even he has stated, thick as two bricks and trying to engage her in conversation is about as interesting as talking to a tea towel; apparently the night-time relations, when he can get it, is very ho-hum. But he got the girl he dreamed of having, the one his friends envied because of her looks and now he's stuck with a girl he can't talk to and doesn't love him the way a wife should. But dang she's good lookin'- and that's all there is. He married the polar opposite, when he knew the type of woman he'd be happiest with all along.

And then my other nut friend who put up with a guy ducking the commitment conversation for 4 years. That's right 4 years. Finally she came right out and asked him at my behest: "are you planning on marrying me one day?" he said "No, no I'm not" and that was the end of that. She never expressed she had dreams of marrying her Mr Right by 32 and having the 2.5 kids with the white picket fence and a dog. And in all that time, he didn't mention that he wasn't going to settle down till after he travelled the world and experienced as many women as he could, on an international scale. He was no oil painting so that was going to take extra time in and of itself.

How people let a supposedly intimate relationship go on so long without knowing each other's aspirations is beyond comprehension. I would expect that should be one of the first things discussed to find if there is true compatibility in mutual desires. Set yourself apart as different even when asking for the same thing and don't wait years to find out. 1-2 years is the most you should wait to talk on this deep level about permanency.

Life has a way of pushing you forward even though you can't see the intended destination. Intuition is your soul speaking to you. Coincidence and synchronicity is your intuition alerting you to the signs, of which you are given to pay attention. Having worked in a spying company – some of the basic jobs were to monitor men and women's behaviour prior to marriage of any suspicion of cheating. One thing I learned and learned quickly was that if you think they're cheating, they most often are. The odd occasion where the partner wasn't cheating was usually clouded by some kind of mental disease, involving paranoia as a symptom of the disease. So if you don't have any characteristics of these diseases, chances are you are going to be right when that gut feeling stirs and tells you something is wrong. Why would a person tell an untrue story unless they have something to hide. Lots of little untruths are often the preliminary of covering up the big lie. Your own body will tell you when something is wrong – it is up to you to trust the signs you are being given. If you have read all the chapters previous to this you will be on your way to learning at least a beginners portion of Handwriting Analysis, Body Language, Talk Language, Micro/Macro Facial Expressions and what you cannot study is good ole Gut Feeling. The collective knowledge of those traits will enable you to trigger that gut feeling, even if you are of the belief you don't have that instinct. You do, we all do. It is in our genes from the dawn of humanity; so how can you not have it. That's the same quality even hunter gathers had when they knew when to go forward with a kill or to retreat because it was too dangerous. There are 3 Phases to Love: Sex Drive /Romantic Love / Attachment. Your intuition is there, it's there, find it and listen to it at any and all stages of a relationship.

When you have been asked/asked someone new on a date, give them tunnel vision to you when at dinner for example – look them face on and look at the bridge of their nose – this will draw in the eye line. This is why often people who have fallen in love will, so to speak, only have eyes for each other and the rest of the world just 'melts away'. It's not that at all – they have such extended eye contact that they only see the other and subconsciously trigger tunnel vision.

There is a condition named after PT Barnham – the circus master; called The Barham Effect – he states 'there is a sucker born every minute' – a famous phrase you may have heard. It relates to The Human Condition and its acceptance of truth even if there is none. Believers in spiritual practises can fall for the: " you have untapped talent you feel you haven't used / you are family orientated / you haven't reached your full potential" type of reading though while one can be lead to believe it relates only to themselves, it indeed relates to many and nearly all people. These are generalisations easily made and in an experiment with a room full of people – they were all given the one astrological reading to which not one member of the room said it was not an accurate description of themselves. It in fact, was the reading of Ed Kemper – a notorious serial killer in the US.

It is often the case you will have intense sexual chemistry with the person who makes your heart race. Wish we could just come right out and say: "are you romantically interested in me?" so we could just get on with it one way or another. You can you know. No-one will ever take that stick and beat you for asking is the rule. The most they will say is no. What have you lost besides worry and indecision caused by the unknown. You will then be able to move on in the direction you are supposed to.

Saying the right thing at the right time in your new relationship also has its merits. Here are some listed for those who think they can't come up with anything poetic by themselves:

"I have romantic aspirations for you that lie just beneath the surface".

"Maybe we could go back to your place and discuss nuclear fusion and its long term effects on the stratosphere" (Be creative).

"You're smart, funny and pretty – you can imagine how happy you make me".

For the boys – always compliment a beautiful woman on her mind and a smart woman on her beauty. In all aspects of your life, try not to state the obvious. Never make a statement to which the obvious response would be "so what".

"I've had an instantaneous attraction to you".

"I'd like .. I'd love.. to kiss you".

"I think about everything about you – the way you sleep, eat, live".

"I have boundaries and limitations that don't accommodate any of those behaviours" (unwarranted behaviour).

"I love you and don't want to be with anyone else".

"Do you see long term potential in this/our relationship?".

Caught cheating: Now would be a good time to ask - "...and what else have you lied to me about?"

Early in a relationship come right out and ask: "do you see yourself falling in love with me" if you need to know where your partner is at.

Allure: Answer a question with a question – "Why do you want to know?"

Communicate with your intimate partners on a level reserved for friends. How sad it is that we share our innermost thoughts and intimate details with our friends but do not disclose these same depths to the one we are most intimate with.

The One is not the person who sets your heart aflutter with nervous tension and indecision. The One should give you the feeling of being completely relaxed and comfortable within your own self. If the person you are with makes you feel nervous and tense, always second guessing yourself – you'll be able to tell if you're being honest with yourself if this is what you have, that this person is far from the right person for you and like a salmon swimming against the current – you too will continue to struggle. Be yourself – be true to yourself and your wants, limitations and shortcomings and the person you attract, when you are the truest version of yourself – you will be loved for you and not the person you are pretending to be. You owe it to others not to falsely advertise. You won't be able to come up with the goods over time and it will all come out in the wash, worth repeating. You can't expect a person to be something other than who they are. That mindset should eliminate disappointment.

In these days of internet dating and the like it is easy to hide behind the facade of the screen's glow. I have been on internet excursions with friends (a friend of mine, not me for real) who met the guy of her dreams on the net and then when we met him he had half his hair and half his teeth and I'm certain he was a good deal older than the 35 he proposed to be. I wanted to say: "and who the eff are you?" when he called her name; but we sat through this dinner (I was the bodyguard/assessor for 1st meetings). What was he hoping for? That they had made such a connection in communications when writing to each other that somehow his altered appearance would be overlooked? Here she's expecting, according to their chats – that he might be The One. You are who you are, you might not be all you can be but there are certain aspects about yourself that you may have difficulty changing, and each person innately knows this about themselves. When a date sits across from you and says 'I have a real thing about cleanliness, it drove my ex nuts' – that is a subconscious disclosure coming out; a warning that must be heeded as they may very well have left off the bit about them, 'freaking out at their partner for leaving so much as a coffee cup on the table'. People will tell you honest assessments of themselves quite unwittingly – listen to them, we are after all our own greatest critics. They are saying it because it's true and somewhere along the line it has had an impact on their lives for them to even mention it. Who would say they party too much and get carried away drinking, if they're home on a Saturday night reading regularly – they won't say it. Pay attention to what people tell you about themselves so three months later you're not saying he acted like a freak when I left the plate on the counter. That warning may well have been there from as early as the first date. And the ole – ' he/she won't be like that to me' – whatever would make you think that someone who has had a behaviour instilled and practised within themselves, all their lives, are going to make an exception and change this behaviour for you. What makes you more special than the person before you and the one before that? Doesn't make an ounce of sense does it. A leopard can't change it spots but people can make a conscious effort to change, it's just that often times they don't or won't do it.

If something is right it will bear good fruit.

Never forget: it's amazing how many wonderful people are still walking this earth.

...and you walk again with your wound.

CHAPTER 7   THE WORKPLACE

The Employee: The single most forgotten factor in most workplaces, unless it's a job deeply loved – is that You Are Being Paid To Be There. Everyone knows for the most part, you are not there for love and your boss most likely knows that. You are being paid to perform at a level worthy of your pay check. Now if you think you are being underpaid for the work you do – in reality that is, then it's entirely a different matter but this book is for the general; thereby assuming that the $20/$30/$40 whatever dollars an hour you may be on – someone is expecting to get their money's worth out of you and the sooner you get with the program – the more pleased the company will be with your performance.

Performance monitoring is something even $15 million dollar contract sports players are subjected to, if they don't come up with the goods, they don't get their contract renewed. It's simple. Now I notice with the new generation of workers – the strong moral structure/work ethic one used to have instilled in them from an early age is missing. In my last job, it was as if they showed up on a Monday or Friday they were doing us all a favour. Well in a nutshell that attitude is going to only get you so far, and will indeed hamper your future prospects, if for example, you were to be let go for tardiness or some other completely controllable reason. What one needs to remember first and foremost is that someone who employs you has expectations of what you will bring to the table and when you do not meet that expectation – the boss will not be happy. No-one is paying for you to search the internet for personal reasons, or play the video sent in emails from your friends. They aren't paying you to stretch out your lunchbreaks or snake in an extra tea or smoke break. This whole doctrine is about doing the right thing, even if no-one is looking. Doing the right thing at work is just as important as doing it anywhere else. It will gain you the respect of your peers and fellow workers. One can mostly only do this by doing a good job. Find out your boss/company's goals and do all you can to focus and contribute to their fulfilment. Someone will notice. And they notice a hellava lot faster if you are shirking your responsibilities.

Make a commitment to do the right thing for the money your being paid and you will be a conscientious employee. An employee I knew would go to the bathroom every morning 10 mins after arriving at work for at least 15 minutes – he did all but take the newspaper in to read. I asked him about this regular occurrence and he said: "I shiet in company time". While it was very funny, the boss mustn't have thought so because that was listed as one of the reasons for letting him go. The other was his constant distraction of other staff. Especially in a sales role, when you're Chatty Kathy at the office – you are costing that employee money. When I was selling advertising and someone would tell some long winded story about their day/life. I would think that

15 minutes just cost me however many dollars. It would help me stay more focused. Don't cost anyone. That's why people who work together sometimes go out for drinks after work on a Friday – to catch up with all the talk that they haven't had the chance to previously. There is a time and place for workplace catch up and it's not Monday morning at your friend's desk or in the kitchen. You'd be amazed how rewarding the feeling of doing a good and conscientious job can be.

You don't have to be a kiss-a$$ about it. The average boss can pick a suckhole up in no time. Don't suck up to the boss, you won't need to if you do a good job and have an awareness of doing the right thing. This book is not titled "Get Part of Your Game Up" – to have good game it has to be on all fronts. If someone trusts you in their employ, you owe it to them to have loyalty and meet the expectations they have of you.

Personally, if an employer of mine 'Trains me' in a skill I previously did not have. If I leave that place of employ I will not work for one of their direct competitors. I may work in the same field or similar but will not contribute to the gain of someone they see as the enemy. That's my contribution to company loyalty. Think of a way you can show your company loyalty and do it. It'll make a difference to the company and you.

Try Hard Don't Work Hard – find the most efficient way of doing your job. Do things right the first time. Save yourself a trip and the chance you may get recognition for being the person whose work never needs redoing.

Remember at all times to be respectful to your superiors and peers alike. Being the office mood-swinger is a reputation that can be a long while in forgiving and forgetting. What it is from 'The Human Condition' perspective side; office interactions seem to be highly judgemental at the smallest slight and easily offended. It is the nature of the person that can do office work and sit in a chair for 8 hours a day, as opposed to the person who has chosen to work outdoors. It is often been said from the 'outdoor worker' – "I could never do an office job and be stuck inside all day" but one very rarely hears from an office worker that they could never work 'outdoors'. Additionally they are indoors all day yet complain about the conditions outside e.g. 'Oh it's raining, it's too hot outside' etc. So herein lies the difference between the two. In or outdoor – you should always be recognised as someone who is polite and personable to be around and extremely efficient at your job.

Regarding being inappropriate with the boss – never, ever, ever do it. Full stop. Employees should not be 'friends' on a social scale with their managers as managers should keep a respectful working distance with their employee.

Work like you don't need the money.

The Manager: The Human Condition is to favour – Parenthood & Professionalism requires it be disguised. If you are in a Management position; that is the first and foremost thing that leads to managerial disfavour from employees. If you can't control how you appear in front of the office deeckhead, try to have as little interaction as possible without failing in your duty of what is required. No-one's going to say 'my boss ignores' me over 'eff he favours so and so'. If, for worst case scenario, you really can't stand the sight of a member of your crew, you must have a Number 2 in position and have that person do most if not all of the interactions.

The formula for getting the most out of your employees is to make them feel proud of what they do and not that they're being overlooked by warlords. The days of the Type A personality manager is all but done away with. You know the type, the one who loses it, yells and stomps and all that carry-on. One could break down the different types of management styles yet here I only encourage one management style - "Attract more Bees with Honey than with Vinegar", it really works as a formula for cohesion and success. Be the type of boss that you would like to have bossing you. Offset the drawbacks of a person's performance with their positives yet all the while pointing it out that they do have drawbacks which need fixing. Managers should have access to employees 'date of births' – read up the sun sign (outer appearances) on each employee and address them accordingly, it will make your life incredibly easier, you'll see the results in a comparatively short period of time. Even in reading up on their sun signs you are sure to recognise their character traits. Taking the time to do this will alter your chances for future success with the individuals under your watch.

CHAPTER 8   THE SOUL & SPIRIT

Regarding transformation - Some things 'are hard' but as Cat Stevens says, 'but it's harder to ignore it'.

Just like violence is a choice, so too is every action you take. Be aware – do no harm.

One has to forgive for their own health and well-being. Even if you haven't come to that, know it needs to be the end result. Anger bleeds; draining you, weakening you. Anger & hatred is your cross to bear.

If you have lived adverse conditions or a painful upbringing or anything of that nature; make it a part of who you are but don't let it define you. It's a part of what you needed to do to be whole within yourself. If you have had adversity in your life – know that it makes you who you are and what you are today and quite possibly, the lessons are intentional for the areas of growth you require. It's not the maker out to get you, it is guiding you. Understandingly, some people have been through tragic circumstances and that might be you, but part of this new place of yours involves letting go of all that is negative. All.

Worse still, when you crutch with another person's negativity, you give them more than they have already taken from you. If parents of murdered children can learn to let go and move on into the future, without ongoing resentment – so too can you. They first hand know not to empower that criminal with more worth than is deserving. The Green River Killer, Gary Ridgeway, an American serial killer, was forgiven by one of his victim's father when he addressed the court in the 'victims' impact statement' time of the trial. What a man that father must have been. Many a religion will direct its followers to forgive, and many advocates of that religion, may find it very difficult to forgive even the smallest sleight. Don't let the toxins of this behaviour affect you. Know that lack of forgiveness affects the forgiver as much as the forgiven. Revenge's joy makes you happy for that one moment in time. It doesn't last. The feeling of emptiness afterwards is an anti-climax. Prepare for it if that is your way.

There is no need to jump to conclusions about a circumstance you need to deal with. Assess it much like a judge would. Be impartial, look at all the facts and whatever sides of the story there are and from whom they came. Then make your assessment based on Reasonable Doubt as to whether the circumstance occurred at all. Beyond Reasonable Doubt is not beyond a Shadow of a Doubt. Collectively; think – before rash judgement; is it possible that this person is perhaps the unluckiest person on this earth that this would happen to them sequentially; or is there a greater probability that you can presume guilt based on the chances of it happening that way. Judges also give a fair, unemotional and impartial sentence, applicable to the crime. If you deal with all your dilemmas in this objective fashion, they will be resolved with the minimum amount of drama. Indulging in drama is the sign of someone with no game; as they are not aware of the need to rise above it.

Know in your heart there is a rhythm and order to these actions and the sinner will indeed pay their penalty in their own time and place. It is Universal Law that will take care of the man who, for example hit a child and drove away, avoiding being accountable for his actions. It could be one of his beloved children will meet an untimely fate, or a spouse, it could be anything but the debt of such a crime will be repaid tenfold.

You don't drive down the street looking into the rear view mirror at what you past – you'll crash. Look ahead to see what's coming, what amazing things might be in store for you. Look forward to the future.

Everything has it's time and place; there is a silent order to this Universe. If you haven't got something you need, deserve or simply want – perhaps it is that you are not ready for it. Some things come in their time. Is it that you want something for the wrong reason/s? If so and you are not suited to it, it may never come. Think of success at an unnaturally high level at an early age, it may make you a drug addict or take on another toxic option to cope with the circumstances. A plethora of child stars could tell you that. Know that you are given all that you need to learn the lessons you have in this life, and which may set you on a path you need to tread to grow. One never learns anything when things are going well, all lessons come in times of hardship and discord. Personally I think I've had enough hard times to build the next Eiffel Tower as far as growth is concerned; but I do not doubt for one second it is these moments in my life, that have shaped me into the person I have become and am today. And if there is such a thing as heaven; I actually stand a chance of getting there instead of being beetchslapped into the ground floor with the burning embers below.

Some cultures believe life is a sequence of circumstances, a preordained path or fate. I'll use the example of a basketball to explain. At the top and bottom all the lines meet. Each line is a path you can choose to travel (choice being the operative word) Let's say, the bottom of the ball is where your life begins. You can travel up any one of those lines; you could even switch paths (lines) along the way and go back and forth to the same line if you want to. How you get from A (the beginning) to B (the end/top of the ball) is purely a matter of your own choice and decisions. If you are on the wrong path you can switch lines on any part of the journey and get back on track but all paths lead to the same definitive end. Life is just like that. If you are not the person you want to be, perusing the things you dream of, or being wrong or bad in any way – there is not one point in your life when you cannot change your thoughts, actions or behaviours to get back on track. The only time it'll ever be too late to change is when you're on your deathbed, and even then some think crying out loud for mercy will be enough. The aim is to not make excuses, just make the change required and get on with putting it into action. Try to make your path the smoothest road possible; instead of choosing one filled with cracks and potholes where it is inevitable you will trip and fall, and cause all sorts of damage and injury to yourself.

To have a broad perspective of familiarity with all aspects of life is imperative to the person flexible enough to fall into the class of having good game. Learn all you can and endeavour to be as broad-minded with that knowledge as it is within reason to be.

The connection we humans have with animals/pets is so strong (to most, not the abusers) as it is devoid of deception and alternate purpose. Animals have no ulterior motive – they are truthful and never lie. This is a relationship of the purest nature. No child should grow up without the benefit of a pet. It is oftentimes the parent that objects and in that objection lies lessons not learnt.

The Universe will control what life lessons a person must learn and you have no place intervening. Leave them to their own fate. As fate, depending on one's actions; can deal a cruel, precise and all-encompassing blow.

Yet if you yourself have been the sinner and have made a conscious choice to change your ways – the opportunity to do so will be presented to you for redemption. It is how you react and if your desire to change is real, that the outcome will show itself. For example; if you have had prior behaviours of theft and stealing, you may get your dream job working in a bank or other financial institution. You may find yourself entrusted with highly sensitive information such as account numbers/residential addresses and the like. You are brought to face your weakness head on and this may be your very last opportunity to change. As this time if you do not steal, you will go on through a safe and secure career with this golden opportunity presented to you. Yet if you do fail – you will go to jail for white collar crime and be convicted of theft in a court of law. Your chance of securing in the future any meaningful job/career which holds responsibility, may not be nil but it will be close to it. The Universe will give you that last opportunity for redemption and it will be solely up to you what you make of it. The outcome being you will be cleared of previous behaviours; or fail and start seeing consequences of your own choosing. Choose wisely whatever your circumstances.

Fully know of the power that lies in your own existence. Look inside not outside to fulfil your needs and answer your own internal questions. It all lies within not externally.

I can't sing in tune so I make up for it in volume. I'm a really bad dancer but that doesn't discourage me in the slightest. As offensive and embarrassing as this can be to my friends, I'm not hurting anyone. And that's all it's really about when it all boils down.

For every action there is a reaction. Liken it to the drop of water in a lake – the circles surround it in reverberation, seemingly endless till it exhausts itself and dies of its own accord. If you do a deed in 'action' – there will be a distinct and definite 'reaction' to what you have done, either for the positive or the negative. The man who does something wrong to his wife is not only affecting her life, but that of the children and, depending on what his action, it may affect the in-laws and grandparents of the children. It never stops at just you unless it is an act of no negative consequence; which usually stems only from an act of love. If you are kind and say a kind word to the sales assistant, for example, you don't know that she may have been contemplating suicide until your kind words to her, on this day – made all the difference in the world. Life has these never ending sequences of events that can come about from the smallest of actions.

For there to be birth there must be death. Love is truly eternal. Love never sleeps. It has been recorded in many medical journals - the event of Near Death

Experiences. Anyone who has had a near death experience will tell you that they know what happens in the end and that they have come back changed beyond anything they ever thought possible. The mainstream channels have had specials on the television, so commonplace is this condition – this is not new news, it is a medical condition cited by the majority of patients whose heart has stopped (predominantly) for an undetermined amount of time, as in those whose heart stopped a little or long while. It is a real experience whether borne from the chemicals activated in the brain upon death, or from what is really there. Look it up – there's research work everywhere about it. The stories vary as to which relative/loved one came to get them yet the outcome of the stories are always the same and they have the same thread of incidences. They all say the same tunnel aspect to the story and an all-encompassing white light that soothes them, and makes them completely fearless of death at the time and upon awakening. Reports state that we are judged by ourselves when our 'lives flash before our eyes'. We are made to answer – ***"What did you do for your fellow man"*** (or variations/themes of that same question) They say they communicate without speaking in 'heaven' – talk, it is all with the mind but they are 100% aware of what messages are being told. They all come back to consciousness with a profound sense of the change in their behaviour if required; there is no other condition nor experience which makes such a profound and permanent change in a person. This change includes how they view the world, what's important in it and how their future behaviour needs to be curtailed. They arise from this experience with a profound change for the better. In the feedback of people who have had Near Death Experiences, the first thing they claim is the monumental life change that comes about after their experience because they all seem to come back knowing when we die, we are not judged by anyone else but ourselves. Whether or not it's a chemical release in the brain as scientists put this experience down to; or the actual experience being the real thing, as people who have had this experience insist.

But what is most noteworthy is not one of them having the fear of death. Not one single one. Some people go as far as to say they welcome death and are disappointed they didn't go this time and had to return to fulfil their life's work. So, if, in the long shot you don't believe it to be the case, Near Death Experiences existing... at the very least it would not hurt you to be prepared and have a good answer for "What have you done for your fellow man?". From the smallest act of kindness to the largest you can spare – do for your fellow man. Contribute.

The question then becomes do you need to get that close to the end to make the changes required to live a full, pure and whole life without any repercussions. Pretend it has happened to you if that's what it takes. Pretend you have been lost at sea for 12 days without food and water, your life is all but over save for the would-be-rescuers you don't know are on the way.

In that life raft, write that note to your loved ones; what would you tell them, have you told them any of these words before? Maybe you should as surely you would regret it if the chance to do so was taken from you. What would you promise the creator (call him whatever name is the prophet of your choosing– Jesus/Buddha/Allah/Mohammed etc.) what would you promise to change if he/she gave you one last chance to stay alive. And make those changes now before they become regrets. Ask anyone who has lost a loved one without the chance to say goodbye, of the list of things they wish they had said, but maybe were too shy or embarrassed to say. Believe it, no-one's going to take a stick and beat you for saying "do you know I love you, I have always loved you as far back as I can remember and I can't imagine my life without you in it." The only person who might take that stick to you, is an ex you're being stalkerish with. Outside of that, it will be music to a loved one's ear and you yourself will live without regret if unfortunate circumstances ever come to pass. No sadder words have been spoken than "I wish I had the chance to tell her (or him)..." – Don't let this be you. Be the best person you can be here and now and let those who are loved by you know it. That alone will bring about an inner sense of peace that all the money in the world cannot buy. Emotional life does not work on credit. Pay it now or accept the chance to gain may be lost to you forever.

Police Forces Use Psychics – they don't do a big song and dance about it but they do. Some psychics are used and regularly so, if they have proved their worth previously, time and again. In the case of John Wayne Gacy; the psychic used, Dorothy Allen, told of the bodies in his house and the arch shape they were buried in much before they were discovered and dug up. One psychic was interviewed and treated as a suspect, such was the knowledge of the body of a nurse, found wrapped in a blue blanket with her white nursing shoes on. A psychic directed one of Linda Soebeck's friends to her handbag disposed of by her killer, which led to retrieval of the car rental record of who committed her crime. There are too many examples to list.

For Past Lives; some studies go as far as to say that unrealistic fears we have in this life is a by-product of a previous life. So too, of the impressionist painter child aged four and the Mozart playing pianist aged 8. Great pianists in their forties have not yet grasped Mozart; it is astounding to see a young boy playing it at the level of the composer himself. Read up on the case histories about this topic also. There are many aspects of life we cannot fathom because of others beliefs imprinted on us, or of how we were taught in school.

What we do come to learn as a part of course, is to waste less time in irrelevant analysis, as we learn to relax and let things be. If one takes the same amount of time and energy spent on worry and anxiety, and converts that into time spent pursuing a goal or passion, your path will be consumed instead with what it is that inspires and fulfils you, instead of what causes you concern. This is a tactic most people naturally grow to understand later in life whether they practised it all along or not. It is a gift that comes with age. Worry begets worry not completion. If one can think of a time when they worried and it concluded with that worry helping their cause – they would be one of the few lucky ones, in a circumstance not once heard of publically as an outcome. What we worry about does not usually turn out as bad as we thought it would be and worry will not change it. The goal in life should be for Harmony and Joy. Neither rises from the ashes of worry. Let things be as they are to be. Cool, calm and collected is a stance not for just particular situations, it is an everyday state of being to be sought and instilled in the self.

People are motivated to eliminate the suffering of other people by their very nature. Somehow humanity has come to the conclusion that it is better these days not to get involved in any others' business/struggle. Surprisingly this is a matter of demographics for a good part. Who would be more likely to help their fellow man – a Texan or New Yorker. The folk in Texas live a very different life than those in NY. New Yorkers know from experience of muggings and heavily inundated crime; that you are just a shot away from being dead, and the chance of finding the perpetrator amongst that vast populous is small. Texans know that other people fear the strict Texas justice system and the death penalty looms near for serious crime. The Rangers there are relentless in their search for a criminal. They stand a better chance of being caught if a crime is committed in Texas. That is not to say the NYPD aren't an efficient bunch, just that the odds are different. An experiment was done whereby an altercation was staged with a gay couple with children dining and another customer mocking them, even the waitress in this experiment took a turn telling the couple of their wrongdoing. Texans by a dramatic percentage stepped up and defended the family with their most common interference being "we're all people". The New Yorkers had a very "I didn't want to get involved" response. Which one could say, can be understandably so. So what does this tell us? That if you live in a safer place, you will be a kinder more compassionate person? No. It tells us that self-preservation reigns supreme over all other decisioning layouts. We are prepared to do for our fellow man when there is no cost to ourselves. Often times the same person who ignored another in distress, also has other attributes which show consistency in that single mindedness. It's more of who we are and what we were taught growing up as to what becomes important in later life.

How can you act like nothing is happening when something is. Silence is a failure. Let it be your humanitarian contribution, to see injustice in any sentient being, and no longer do nothing. You will feel enriched by these actions. Imagine if everyone just did their bit – nothing more, nothing less. Just your bit. There'd be no bits left to do.

Some have the belief system that there is a fixed and natural order to the Universe. Signs – accidents – fate – serendipity, they all play a part. Once you keep your mind open to signs or symbols of a burning question or path you may take etc. the signs literally scream out at you. For example: If you're looking at buying a house on 5th Avenue and are still unsure, you may see the number 5 repeated in a random series of coincidences, that you just can't explain how they all came together. For example, when looking to buy a house – the address was 12 Green Street... the same number and amount of letters of my sister's house, I was having something professionally painted and the painter came to me with 5 shades of green on a colour palette. I saw 12 crows fly overhead the day I went for a second viewing (in the dark – not recommended)...and the repetition went on and on. When I moved into the house with, what looked in winter like dead trees for a front garden, when springtime came within a short while, the dead trees were rose bushes that blossomed into the same sequence of colours, which were viewed from the front window of my house in America. That set my mind at ease that this was the right place for me. Serendipity does share a path with us and it is just a matter of how aware you may be, to receiving the messages which sometimes are so apparent, if it was a snake it would have bitten you. Keep your mind open.

All mistakes connects back to the one nexus - Haste. Don't be hasty in your decision making. Take your time. If time is of the essence, think clearly before jumping in. If it is something that is right – it will come to you.

Have you ever met someone you would class as a 'Wise Soul?'. They seem to have a radiant and free spirit. Some aspects of the wise soul are readily visible in some children.

Having worked in the criminal justice system, I hated what I saw. It's like a victim loses their life on the day that crime was committed – so too does their family. You can tell just by looking at them, they will never be the same person again. A murderer kills much more than the person they hurt. They kill the loved ones of the deceased, who too, become victims.

Be a Good, Honest, and Ethical Person. You won't put a foot wrong that way. Learn Compassion. Learn to treat all beings equally but in a dissociative manner. Love without the pain attached to it. Love like you are aware there is a beginning and end to all things, and the cyclical effect of life & death is expected.

What we do to other living beings is also a strong part of our soul's satisfaction. What I find particularly galling is when the Black Rhino was declared officially extinct on 14th of November, 2011 is that poachers took this animal's whole body for the sake of its horn, supposedly a powerful aphrodisiac. Says who? Who stepped up and said it actually worked - this archaic belief? Any one person? No. Not one said it. Helluva if you wanted to get 'horny' – drink alcohol. That'll do it every time; to the point that when antibiotics were first invented for syphilis and other sexually transmitted social diseases – the original warning of "do not drink alcohol with antibiotics" was solely for the reason of getting footloose and fancy free, and spreading disease further. Everyone who has drunk alcohol on antibiotics will know – nothing bad came of the combination (of course I'm not recommending this). These future generations are going to be cross at our generation for knowing what was going on and choosing to ignore it to the point of extinction. If we gave even the smallest portion of the budget set aside for the Iraqi war, which was used to kill people – and gave that amount to the conservation of saving species on the brink of extinction – we would have no species facing extinction. Or if that same budget was spent on stopping famine worldwide, imagine the impact that would make. Now if that's not a sad state of affairs I don't know what is. Wiping out an entire species because of some misguided belief in the power of its horn or leaving our own to starve. It's not right, it's not ethical, and it's not acceptable in any measure. It is akin to animals having a fetish for hairless skinned people – we'd be wiped out too. Whales would be swimming around in t-shirts that read: "Save the people". It's not a weakness or a softness to have respect for all living things – it's a duty; including our duty to each other's well-being. Human beings are historically war-mongers and control freaks.

FUTURE GENERATIONS WILL WANT TO SEE THESE CREATURES ALIVE AND IN THEIR NATURAL HABITAT.

Which choice would an animal take if given one – a 6x8 crate or a 10 hectare habitat in nature? For this reason, as many have supported, circuses are all but a thing of the past. I have seen elephants roaming free and none of them were wearing a tutu, nor were they following each other holding their tails. Not one of them did a mindless trick to entertain me. Humans have their desires monopolise the entire planet... and if a shark bit them while they were swimming in their wilderness, they eliminated them in droves as an act of revenge. Thankfully this too, is a thing of the past and in some endangered areas the sharks habitat became protected (Some Australian states & South Africa to name two) What we don't realise is that it takes up to 7-10 years for this species to reproduce and the sharks caught in the nets these days are, at best, mostly around 7. Ask the Hawaiians what happened when they wiped out the Tiger Sharks after a string of attacks: everything else slowly follows and other predators, not in the apex section of the food chain, multiply out of control as seals did, dirtying its beaches and affecting tourism. Do we really need the palm oil from the Orangutans habitat – or the mahogany wood that is wiping out the Chimpanzee territory? We'll soon find out what happens and what effect it has on us, when living without the apex predator. When to say 'when' is here and now. The way we treat nature is unsustainable and has been for a long while now.

In the scheme of things – We are All God's Children; I am of the belief that God's gonna kick your a$$ when you get up there if you've done anything to hurt his children or his creatures. There is something so innately wrong with someone who could harm a defenceless creature including, but not limited to, a child. It is the most unforgiveable act and one could imagine the oppressive karmic repercussions a debt like that would incur.

It is overwhelmingly apparent that global warming will take a hefty toll on the planet. With the polar ice sheets melting at an alarming rate. If you observe earlier documentaries of the poles you will see an occasional polar bear out in the water or floating amongst sheets of ice. Now if you watch a documentary of the same area, you can see up to eighty polar bears in the water and bare sheeting. It's visible – the damage we have caused and how grim things are. Having heard the Australian Prime Minister say he was cutting emissions by 5% - I felt like writing to him – " Have you lost your whole head? " Yeah that's not gonna cut it buddy-o. Carbon Dioxide is at the highest level it's been in two million years. Sir David Attenborough has referred to Man as The

Super-Predator. All life is precious, it does not matter which form it takes.

When you raise an animal you are responsible for its destiny. Choose wisely when considering pet ownership. Dogs are pack animals and when we lock them outside or have 'an outside dog' we are segregating them from their pack and more often than not, this is the largest contributor and prerequisite of bad behaviour. It is the first question to be asked when someone speaks of their barking, hole digging, misbehaving pooch. If you want an outside animal – get a goat or sheep or chickens – any animal that won't live a life of depravity from your personal choice based on carpets, wood flooring or shedding hair. I won't comment on indoor cats, lest my house be burned to the ground. Just know that you can live in a castle and you will still want to go outside. Cat runs and add-ons are ideal for this situation. Letting a cat roam free allows it to incorporate other aspects of living that could kill it. Having had a cat hit by a car - anyone's who's been through that will tell you they don't want to go through it twice.

The soul food of the self requires us to lose the Facade or Shadow Side of ourselves. Or at the very least, cease the negative side of you. A perfect example of the shadow side is the double life of Vincent Brothers. The mild mannered Vice Principle who, after the work day of looking after and being entrusted with primary school children – would go home and abuse his wife and terrorise his own children. He was ultimately convicted of murdering Joanie, their 3 children and his mother-in-law. To look at him from his daily life one could never believe the dark side that existed within him. He was indeed two separate personas. Be one whole person instead of altering your nature to the company you keep. Make yourself 'First Amongst Equals'.

Do you tell others about these shining moments in your life that require changing; you don't have to. They are of the past, and no longer exist as a future possibility. They have no place in the present and thereby there is no benefit from dredging them up. Unless, of course, you are a thief going for a job in a financial institution or the like. Within reason, leave the past well enough alone. Let the dead dog you have committed to not resurrecting, lie.

If you had something to do over again – sure you'd do it differently but it's no secret we don't have things to do over. You never have it to do over. Do things and act with the knowledge that you may never pass that way again.

Be a participant in life – not an observer. It will enrich your life to engage. Things may not always turn out the way planned, but trial and error exists as do the lessons that come of it.

Be Kind. Be good to each other and take care of each other – your creator expects it from you. How could anyone in Western Australia forget Andrew Pea who was stabbed some forty times (that could be exaggerating that figure but I don't think so) on a bridge in the middle of the city I grew up in - maybe it was forty people who watched and did nothing. Forty is in there somewhere; I was incredulous at the news even as a teenager. I know I would have done something, even back then before my hideous beatings with life lessons – I would have helped Andrew Pea. One shouldn't need a Good Samaritan Law to guide us to what is right to do to our fellow man. When a young guy on a train, sitting in the elderly seat turns up his IPod and looks down as the eight month pregnant or elderly lady gets on – well you just know I turn into the 'transport monitor'. If we stand by and watch injustice we are in part to blame for allowing it to be. It's the same concept as the biggest lies are told with silence. Inaction being the equivalent. Non-action is as bad as helping the act along.

Be true to yourself – it will keep your spirits high. If you are being dishonest, know that there are no degrees of honesty. Either you are being honest or you are not. Only psychopaths don't know the difference.

A good start is to begin to smile and make eye contact with the man/woman in a wheelchair, or those who have other outward signs of having a disability, or show a difference to what you deem as 'normal' or 'mainstream'. Think of how many people have averted their eyes or shown they were awkward or uncomfortable when in their company. Someone once told me she 'would rather people ask what's wrong with her than to stare. They stare or they look away' – there seems to be no in between. Kindness sees no difference, change this about your behaviour today if you have been guilty of this in the past. Regardless of what religion one belongs to – we are all gods' creatures. Make kindness an everyday thing.

Don't leave your footprints – move on freely and without shackles. When one ends a relationship with war and discord, that person becomes mentally attached to you; whether the memory of them brings feelings of anger, or hatred, whatever the negative feeling. You can walk away from a relationship without any of this if you make peace with the person, mentally release them with well wishes and then move on. The thing is if you have gone through your life hurting people that is like entrapping yourself to them – either by thought or deed, if you have a conscience (back to psychopaths being the only ones who don't) then that deed or action should haunt you. Sincerely apologise and even if they don't forgive you - you will set your soul free from that attachment. You must obtain this peace of mind and clear old grievances as best you can if you are to move on with a free and light heart.

Action / Reaction: Be aware that this is a part of cyclical change and course. Be gentle with your actions and the same reactions will follow suit. You can redeem yourself, even if you have been a complete and utter (bleep) your whole life. If you plan a course to consciously fix things – you will redeem yourself in the eyes of those around you, they'll wonder what the hellava happened to your (bleep) self, as change is always noticeable. Life's too short to spend it with nasty people. Anger is an attempt at control. Guilt is one tool used to action that control.

Know that the best way to win an argument is to disengage. Make your point firmly and without emotion. When you are right, you don't need to prove a point you already know is correct. Do not engage in an argument about it. Furthermore, don't let people bully you into anything that you don't want. Say to them 'You might be able to bully other people that way but you can't bully me.'

Meditation: Make a conscious effort not to hold your breath in times of stress and worry (we do it subconsciously so you have to consciously be aware of it). Meditate – thoughts will interrupt – let them flow and pass and concentrate on your breathing again. The time will come where you can control the random soliloquy of noise that goes on inside your mind. Endeavour to not think. Listen to your breathing.

Count the breaths "In – two – three – four. Hold – two – three – four. Out – two – three – four. Hold Exhale – two - three – four.

When you have breathed out and are in the phase of the last hold after the exhale, when you have no breath in your body; they say this is the closest we come to what death feels like. When you have reached a deep level form of meditative state – it sure feels like this could be so. You will know.

When you are past the early learning stages of meditation as a practise start Creative Visualisation. Picture your life as you wish it. Live it like it has already happened and be grateful to Your Maker or whoever you pray to. Creatively Visualise every last exact step of what you aim to achieve; and your reaction (joy etc.) to the successful achievement of your goal. It will come to pass if it is in your higher good to have it. Think of all the things you wished for that you didn't get and in hindsight would have been the worst path your life might have taken. The long term agenda not thought through.

All those tennis players that struggle with their serve. If they only start creative visualising, they would see the difference immediately.

Life & Death: Be kind. Be good to each other - When you lose a husband, wife or some significant other to death or disease – nothing else matters. "What if...What could..." none of any of it can bring them back and nothing else matters in relation to that one thing. Let go of guilt.

Try to keep up hope even when reality and human nature kicks in and you begin to silently question if this is going to be a bad blow and is the hope you hold out false. Hope in and of itself can be quite cruel but hold out for hope until reality tells you otherwise.

My favourite Atheist, in a true spot of bother, asked me to ask God to help her (That still makes me laugh). Quite expectedly I answered, "Ask him yourself". And she did because she had nowhere else beyond herself, to turn. Things ended up turning out for the highest good of all, as do most situations.

Bad luck is not just a play of the cards – a bad draw. There are lessons to be had in that opportunity for growth, and if you are not paying attention you will be made to repeat the lesson again till you 'get it'. Personally, and according to my calculations only, I have had enough growth experiences to build a Mount Everest Base Camp; yet I still find myself occasionally with the: 'oh ok here we go again' thang going on. No-one is exempt.

The Sanskrit saying: A Beautiful Mistake – whereby the worst of the worst experiences are just a beautiful mistake. When someone you love dies, the lessons you learn come hard and fast which is where the beauty in that mistake comes from. It is a mistake that they died so young etc. but it is not an incident to be thrown away from life's lessons. See the negative things in your life as just that; something learnt from a beautiful mistake. Come to regret only the things you haven't done – not the things you have.

From a mental piece perspective - Don't put all your eggs in one basket, nor in one nest. Spread your assets so if one crumbles, it is only a portion that affects you. Anyone who's wanted to throw themselves off something high when the stock market takes a blow, will confirm that this is a good strategy.

You don't have to have a Near Death Experience to evolve with a new level of connecting with others and display altruistic beliefs and behaviours. Feel privileged in the life you have and the opportunities presented to you along the way. Be grateful.

We are entitled and guided to learn to question things that are questionable. Back to the example of the NASA Moon Landing, conspiracy theorists have the right to want answers to why there is a flag waving on a moon with no air. Why are there no stars in space all of a sudden? How is it that we hear the astronaut's voice so clearly amidst silence when there is a giant rocket ship landing? Where's the impact crater where the craft landed? Why is there not even a speck of dust on those footprints when there was a rocket thrust that took place? How did they pass the Van Allen Radiation belt 6 miles deep without the same radiation burns suffered by future astronauts who had travelled into space? NASA were still having incidences with astronauts and rockets exploding in the nineties yet thirty years before they made a first attempt perfect mission. What's with the shadows cast in all directions when there is only one sun shining – in this modern day we call that 'lighting', where is the exhaust plume of the spacecraft as it takes off... the list goes on. The one time I saw a NASA representative address these obvious flaws – his final answer, without any explanation or answer to any of the above asked questions, stated: "The bottom line is NASA sent astronauts to the moon in 1966 and that's it." That's what – why don't you just answer the questions? Give a sound and solid explanation and these so called nuts won't be hounding you with a 'please explain'. Just looking at the background discrepancies alone and the photographic crosshairs behind objects in photos instead of in front – makes for an optically incorrect illusion. You all can do your own research and question the things that don't make sense to you, in any questionable circumstances. In this one instance, I can see why people would question the NASA space mission's authenticity – could Man have landed on Area 51 with their 40 million dollar budget. After all one of the favourite sayings of the 60's = "If you can't make it – fake it." Question what you find in disarray – following as a blind sheep is the other route and not one which someone with game would take. Gullibility becomes no-one.

Question what you find in disarray

The Body: Concentrate on the beauty within: Humans have the trait of vanity which no other living creatures, including dolphins and the great apes, our closest comparisons, do not have. In this pursuit of perfection we attempt all types of changes to make us better. What is the true need for this? What is the true benefit of this? There is none. If you are concerned with looking young and it really affects you, to the point of ongoing dissatisfaction – use Retin A (for anti-aging/repair) at night on your face and sunscreen in the morning with a standard moisturiser in between. It will take up to 12 months to see the full and complete benefit. Tests show that a quality (not expensive) moisturiser daily works every bit as well as those overly expensive face creams that promise the world. Facial Peels are medical acid. Botox is a Botulism toxin. Herbal detox is good for you even though it can taste revolting.

Life can be basic: Getting fit gets rid of fat. Treat your body right. Self-help is about helping yourself and not about playing the victim.

Eat Fat to Lose Fat (Good Fats) – Eat 5 small portion meals instead of 3 large meals.

Use the 80/20 Rule = 80% Good Food & 20% Treat. Keep your favourites for the day you have your 20% treat. Then you won't feel like you are depriving yourself. Exercise: If you brisk walk 30-45 mins 3 x week your body will dramatically improve everything.

Drink water / Add Vegetables – Fish – Seeds to your diet.

Avoid Sugar/ Alcohol increases sugar level.

Don't drink two consecutive nights. Don't drink more than two glasses – drink with a meal.

Fish/Meat/Chicken & Salad or Fish/Meat/Chicken & Vegetables for dinner – No carbs (breads/pasta) and it will assist you in dropping weight and make keeping weight off easier.

Give yourself a break – force yourself to go out into the sunshine for a minimum of 15 minutes per day. Vitamin D is good for you.

Smoking/Excessive anything – you know by now is bad for you. You must take every measure in your power to cease the habit/s entirely. Demons that they are. If you have cut down smoking to even one cigarette a day – then you still have a habit of smoking one cigarette a day.

Live the lifestyle in this book and you will live with a healthy body, peaceful mind, understanding heart and a free soul. The richest of livelihoods will become yours.

SILENT CHAPTER: ANCIENT CIVILIZATIONS

"Keep your mind open and always continue to learn"
(Buddhist Monk)

If you have no interest in this chapter feel free to bypass it. If nothing else; it will give good conversation fodder for the next time you wish to appear worldly, well-read or broad minded.

That we as a species can claim to both understand and for some great part know what is going on with our world, our universe and us as beings on a whole – is ridiculous. If there are 50 million solar systems out there just like ours could it really possibly be that we are the most intelligent form of life in all the depth of space. Just think too of the following topics, and then think some more if you wish. None of these examples are that of my opinion – they are evidenced fact.

Can you imagine if anything alien was exactly like us – we control everything from the life of other species to the quality of air we live in. Imagine how bad a thing that would be for the rest of the universe and to think, that this behaviour would be the only possible, in this vast universe of a million sextillion stars. How is that possible – even our scientists acknowledge that this cannot be so. They are the first to acknowledge it and spend millions of dollars in research monies looking into space for evidence of life on other planets.

The Pyramids at Giza could have found the manpower to be built from hunter/gatherers but they didn't have the knowledge to build them; so precisely that they are 1/10th of a millimetre off True North (the North Pole). Where would they have learned this knowledge of astronomy, geography, mathematics and physics to build structures such as these, which have survived the hands of time? Who then, with what knowledge, built all the other series of pyramids in Mexico, Guatemala, and as far away as underwater off the coast of Japan; where a giant monolith of a face, similar to that of The Sphinx lies beneath the water? As well as the striking resemblance from the photos taken of the moon which show pyramid shapes and pathways.

The Pyramids at Giza are in direct alignment to the constellation of Orion right down to the Milky Way parallel to the Nile, in the year 10,500bc which was when we had the Stone Age and hunter-gatherers. Some theorists suggest the Egyptians were graffiti artists that claimed the tombs inside as their own; who went on to write their names and generations of directives on the walls. How did the peoples of this most primitive of times, have the knowledge to erect these great structures; if indeed they did build them and to which, we in our advanced state – cannot replicate in accuracy a pyramid 6 feet high. The ancient civilizations shared a body of knowledge with us. It shows to build Pyramids and other monolithic structures that we, in science, geography, physics and astronomically cannot duplicate in this modern day and age. Where did this body of knowledge come from and where did it go?

How can one go their entire lives and not question what caused this and how these things came to be?

Even in modern day medicine, our tools are very similar to the ancients, who performed complex brain surgeries, fixed broken bones, could do eye surgery and cosmetic dentistry; with precise instruments; all with tools that our modern day surgeons recognise. Modern day medicine is a reinvention of what the ancients practised; Roman doctors' instruments were carved on their tombs. Gaelan the father of Sports Medicine used ointments and massage and surgery. None of the gladiators treated by him died. Hippocrates was a Greek doctor. Asclepius is the Greek God of Medicine, whose staff and snake symbol are the internationally recognised symbol of medica.

How is it that hunter-gatherer Egyptians built stone structures that our modern day technology cannot replicate? What knowledge did they have that we no longer possess? The question to ask is: How is it that the pyramids at Giza are the most accurate structure to true North, South, East & West, at a time when mankind was at its most primitive. The three pyramids are in perfect alignment with the constellation Orion in 10,500bc, including the Nile and The Milky Way – in a time well before human inhabitation, which is truly a Wonder of the World.

We still haven't found the missing link that shows the origin of man from apes. Ancient Sumerian tablet texts dated from 5000bc describe an alien race who came to earth and show the first modern human beings and where modern man originated from. An incredible notion by any stretch, yet we have evidence of ancient Egyptians, Tutankhamen and his sister – with their elongated skulls, many more of which have been found in all corners of the globe and amongst all ancient civilisations.

Past reveals the future: The Mayan / Nostradamus / Incas – their writings all show of incidents that have taken place in our modern day world. They can't all be flukes.

Question what you find in disarray or nonsensical.

How can we be alone if the question be asked. The galaxy is 10 million years old. We are the youngest intelligence in the Universe; any scientist will tell you that. To know there are millions of galaxies and all the evidence of intelligent civilisations, there may be numerous alien civilizations. Not saying they have to walk, talk and have eyes and ears like us. They may be microscopic capable of reproduction on a desolate, distant planet, that we couldn't even fathom life of any sort existing on. As in being not of earth, we know there is space and objects 100,000's light years away, some four trillion kilometres in the cosmos away from us. How can there not be other life forms? It is statistically improbable that there are no other beings, however large or small, in the millions of star systems out there. There is such a magnificent amount of time and space continuum, it could be that we are just one of the species. We are being ignorant to think we are the only life forms in this magnitude of space that surrounds us. We barely understand our own existence much less that of all in the universe. It was once described to me; 'that it would be madness if you thought your house and your street was the only one in the world' and that parallels can easily be drawn with that mindset of thinking.

If you look at the pyramids in Tiahuanaco, and the size of the stones that form the structure - you can clearly see this is not man-made motion, but rather a knowledge of a practise we in the 21st century fail to grasp. The bricks that form the pyramids at Giza are so big that the ramp theory makes no sense. The stones laid at Machu Pichu are twice the size as that of Giza, and the air up there could not support the workforce they say it would have taken to build. So where does that leave us? With another ramp theory. Is it possible then that higher-minded beings helped mankind?

There is Coral Castle in Florida built by Ed Leeskalnin, a frail and small man who not only formed the giant stones into carvings that can be moved with the push of a finger, but also moved them under the cover of darkness when he relocated, so they ran parallel to the electromagnetic field of the earth. Ed knew something that the same people knew who built the pyramids, he answered the question of 'How he built' his monument to his love who never came after years of waiting for her; with that same answer – "I know how the Pyramids were built" he would openly and freely state every time asked – is this possibly a knowledge of an ancient civilisation, information over time that has been lost and forgotten to our modern civilised race. Florida's called Coral Castle built in 1940, where giant monoliths and coral stones were erected solely by this one man. Ed Leeskalnin, a five foot tall, 100 pound man. He changed his location on to a grid line where and with a higher level of electromagnetic energy, occurred in its natural form, required to complete his project, his labour of love. With love conquering all and everything – how did this frail man erect such immovable objects; in such alignment that one of the pieces can be moved on its axis by one's finger. He never changed his response: he 'knew the secrets of how the Ancients built the pyramids and if he could learn them so can you'.

Think of the folklore of Greek Gods; did our ancient ancestors view aliens as gods. The temples of Greece were built to worship gods – stories told of the origin of the gods who travelled to earth from the skies. From 3800bc Sumerians' text say: 'those from heaven who have come to earth' and depicted in carvings 'supernatural beings interacting with humans. Was it they who became their gods'? Mount Olympus was the home of the gods. Zeus with his thunderbolt weapon sat on his throne and determined the fate of mortal men. The trident weapon of Poseidon was not just a pitchfork; could it have been a direct energy device? Apollo 'rode the skies in his chariot of fire'. There is a description of 'a rumbling with Mt Olympus where the entire top lifted off'. Was this a description of a craft taking off as opposed to a volcanic eruption being described?

The Karnak stones have been dated 4500-2500bc and are the largest collection of standing stones in the world. 350 ton stones and giant megaliths, arranged in intersecting lines that form triangles only visible from above the earth. This unique geometric formation is not a coincidence of 2860 meters, or its half angles being the same geometrical pattern from Stone Age people, that perfectly represents pen-thagaris triangle. Things made in 20bc that can be seen from space. Electromagnetic fields were used as the energy to move giant stones, is as much as we know thus far. Ancient Alien theorists believe extra-terrestrial knowledge was taught to our ancestors, and humans made these giant structures from the instructions of the extra-terrestrial intelligence.

Worldwide the stories remain very similar: Norse mythology has the same theme of supernatural beings and other worlds. They describe powerful gods the same as Roman and Greek gods who do the same things – Odin and Zeus – sky father gods or Divine entities. Weapons of the same descriptions, Odin with his spear/ hammer. Thor/ Zeus parallel with the thunderbolt. Ancient Hebrew texts have a prophet that 'travels the skies' Inhop who 'the lord took him away into a fiery chariot in the heavens'. All ancient civilisations viewed as all 'life came from the sun' and that was recorded through early times. Even Christianity texts speak of David and Goliath, where Giants were found in Nevada, bones in caves of giant creatures who scientists say cannot be human, these bones found of 7-8 foot tall people. Shards of pottery were found from the same time period, of which the name Goliath is engraved in the pottery. Dorman, Europe and the Middle East have located giant's graves – shaped like the Greek letter pie – on top of the upright stone of the Bronze Age, are made by giants or it is that these are just metaphors. Theorists say how these genetic freaks came about, a creation passed on of genetic alterations. They say aliens changed the genetics of early DNA of people and this is how we were created. Tablets depict experiments with human DNA and refer to the Greek Cyclops and images and stories of such creatures.

Considering even Darwin in The Origin of Species, speaks of natural selection, yet he cannot explain the developmental gap of ape to man. In a few thousand years our brain size tripled in volume, which is a relatively short time period on the earth. It jumpstarted human evolution. So where is that missing link in all the things we have discovered over time, could it be that the missing link maybe somewhere outside of where we're looking? Sumerians records clearly have recorded that the first human beings were genetically engineered. It was then that mistakes produced monsters and giants – they recorded the origin of man as such.

In 3000BC the pyramids began to be built – what sped the advancement of human beings, could it be this genetic intervention ancient civilisations all refer to; and are we their product, with all the capabilities common of this time such as Mental Telepathy, Levitation and the like.

Mankind is fulfilling its own doomsday prophecies in accordance with how we behave and treat the earth. If we do not change the behaviours driving this downward pattern, we ourselves ensure the fulfilment of the ancient prophecies. Few believe it will be a solar burst that gets through the hole in the mega sphere (furthest sphere – past the stratosphere) which wipes out our electrical capacity for as much as 2 years. We already are in the 20 year war Nostradamus refers to (Iraq - retreated but still have soldiers there), and the floods, volcanic eruptions and earthquakes spill the blood of the people one hundred fold.

So what then do you do with this newfound knowledge - you look up and verify the evidences I have listed here – and then you figure out your own conclusions. The point is there's so much in this world going on that we haven't skimmed the surface of knowing its origins. It is our path to explore – ask questions, at the very least you'll make great dinner company for being able to talk of such things. That we know more of space than we do of our own ocean still does not attest to much. The Nazi party and their experiments with 'The Bell' and the documented attainment by America of their rocket scientists, along with the other half going to Russia upon the German defeat of WW2. Project Paperclip detailed the vast work these scientists did in contributing to the future of space exploration – it's all documented fact. Right down to the discovery of the smallest thing, The Atom and subsequent building of the Atomic Bomb. Where did all this knowledge originate.

A tall blonde man once told me – "The world is like a book – if you don't travel, you don't get past the first page". The same goes for knowledge and learning. You won't be past the first page if you don't keep up with current affairs, much less things of greater conversational substance. Make it your business to be able to talk about a wide and varied group of subjects, not in a boastful way but in the type of way that could save a really dull evening. Do everything you can to learn those 5 minutes on each topic you think you may ever have to relate to. I can talk about golf and near on any sport – & I dislike sports but predominantly, one gender of the world's populous appears overly interested in it. Herein lies the willingness to learn of something that interests me as much as a story about a hernia, yet I've sat and yakked about it more times than I care to count. It's not about being fake or misleading – we'll just call it being broadminded. All things are relative to the situation at hand. Being able to speak of ancient history and its goings-on on multiple levels, will give the impression that you are well read and knowledgeable about the distant past.

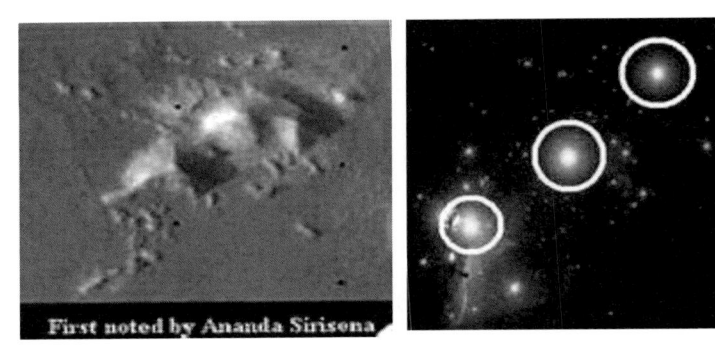

First noted by Ananda Sirisena

PYRAMIDS OF GIZA/ MOON SURFACE PICTURES/CONSTELLATION ORION

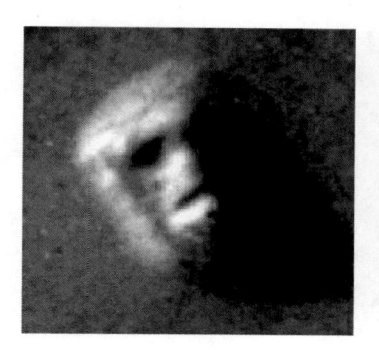

FACE ON MARS/SPHINX/JAPANESE UNDERWATER PYRAMIDS ALSO HAVE A SUNKEN MEGOLITH WHICH CLOSELY RESEMBLES THE FACE OF THE SPHINX

CHICHEN IZA – MEXICO / JAPANESE UNDER-
WATER PYRAMIDS

CORAL CASTLE:

All different cultures from all over the world mimicked the Elongated skull. Nefertiti, Akhenaton, Tutankhamen - their son and all their children had elongated skulls. It can be one of two things – revered and positioned to be like someone they admired as we do today in modern times; or 'extra-terrestrial DNA' is the explanation of Erich Von Daniken, a world renown researcher in the field of Ancient Civilizations and how they came to be and be built. There are many stories from Ancient Greece and Romans that say the 'gods came down from the heavens and their virgin women were impregnated' (in short). We think this unusual yet we today, can impregnate a woman without intercourse or a man. The buildings and structures built in ancient times are so much more advanced than anything our knowledge holds today. It then brings into question whether the ancients were just as advanced in the course of artificial insemination, a milestone we have only just reached. Furthermore, how do we explain who these star gods were that All ancient civilizations say came. No matter which continent one researches, they all say the same thing. To whom do they refer to having this 'star knowledge' - creators and protectors, these supernatural beings. Are their petroglyphs carved in stone, their drawings of what was seen and then depicted in prehistoric wall carvings as visitors from the skies, in much the same way we replicate in modern times (art / paintings / bodily adornment).

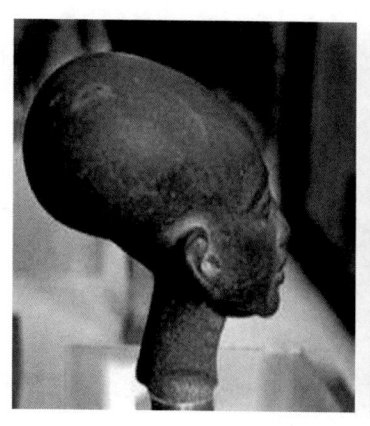

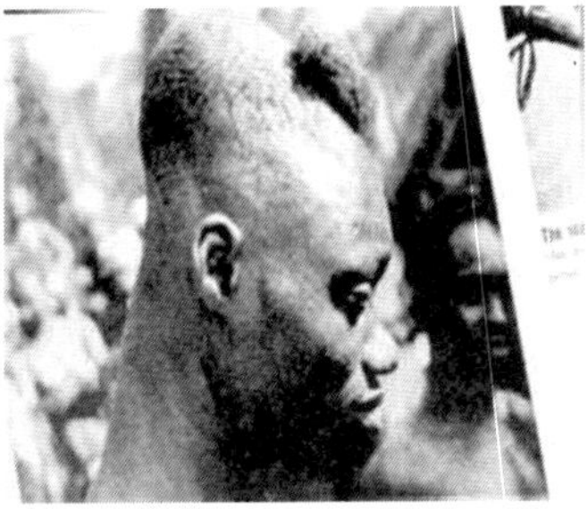

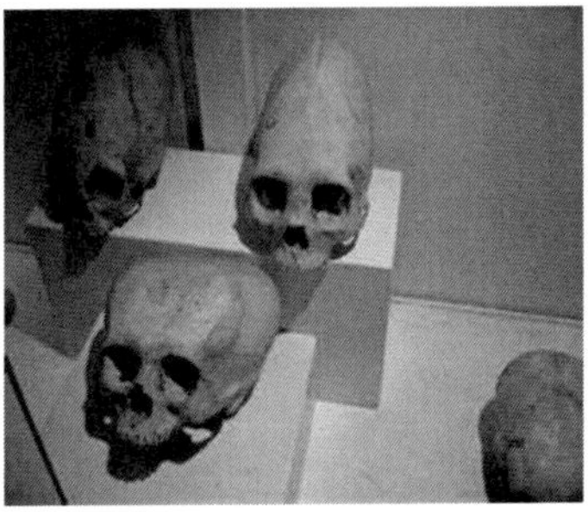

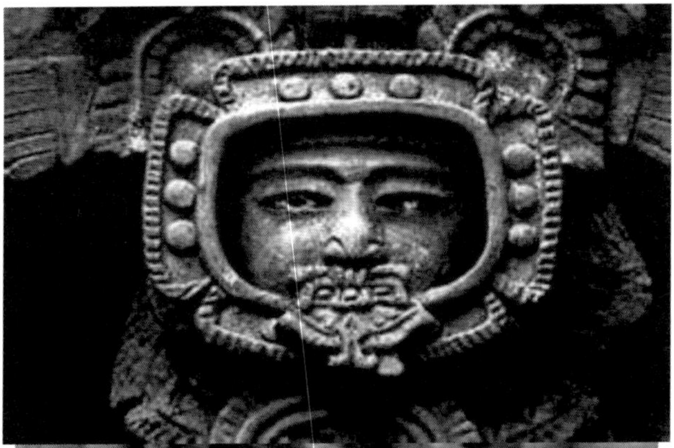

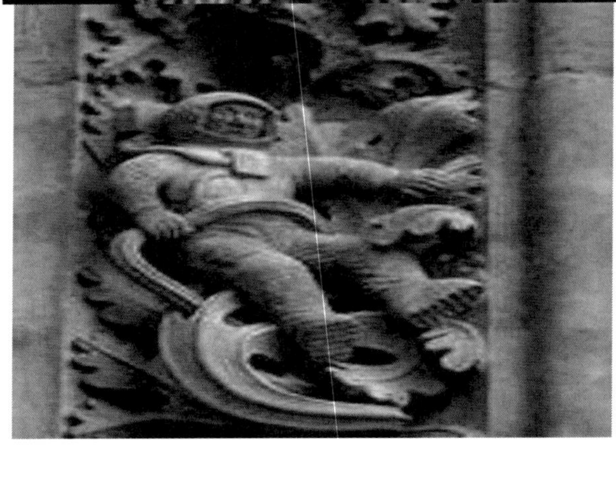

MAYAN AND EGYPTIAN

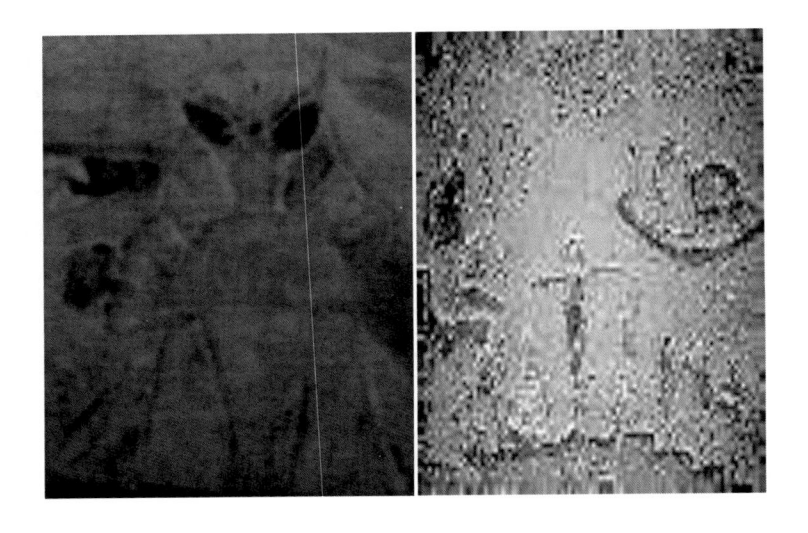

Damaidi

Yugoslavia

Are these records of a previous civilisation from a higher state of mind? Have they recorded and left these monuments and depictions for us to find; so we too may discover the same body of knowledge.

I have inserted this article exactly as is so there is no discrepancy in its meaning. It is of a planet found, quite near earth, which has water and air just like ours and openly states, scientists could have been wrong about no earth like ours. The article quotes the man who discovered the planet called Gliese 518:

Being first isn't the main reason Vogt is excited, however. "Someone had to be first," he says. "But this is right next door to us. That's the big result." What's particularly big about it is a matter of simple arithmetic. With only 116 stars closer to Earth than this one, it was hardly a sure thing that so small a sample group would produce two habitable planets, including Earth. And two such planets may be an undercount, Vogt says, since just nine out of those 100-plus stars have been studied in any detail. Indeed, one of Gliese 581g's sister planets, known as Gliese 581d (O.K., they don't put a lot of creative energy into naming these things), could conceivably be a habitable world itself.

One of the four planets known to orbit Gliese 581 before the latest discovery, 581d was found by a team of Swiss astronomers in 2007 and was thought to be outside the habitable zone and thus too cold for liquid water. But a reanalysis last year brought it into the zone, albeit just barely. The problem is, 581d is too big to be Earthlike; it's probably made mostly of nonwater ice, like Neptune and Uranus, which makes a poorer candidate for life than 581g.

Lost in the excitement over possible life on the new world is what a remarkable achievement its mere discovery was. Detecting a planet this small is monstrously hard — and would have been impossible when Vogt and co-discoverer Paul Butler of the Carnegie Institution of Washington first got into the planet-hunting game in the early 1990s. The instruments you use to detect tiny back-and-forth motions in the star — motions caused by the orbiting planet's gravitational tugs, which are often the only way to infer that the worlds exist at all — simply weren't sensitive enough. Since then, says Vogt, "I've been busting my gut to improve the instruments, and Paul has been busting his gut to do the observations." In all, those observations span more than 200 nights on the giant Keck I telescope in Hawaii over 11 years, supplemented by observations from the Geneva group — and that painstaking work finally confirmed 581g's existence.

None of this proves that there is water on Gliese 581g. "Those are things we just have to speculate about," says Vogt. But he goes on to point out that there's water pretty much everywhere else you look. "There's water on Earth," he says, "and on the moon, and Mars, and on Jupiter's moon Europa and Saturn's moon Enceladus, and in interstellar space. There's enough water produced in the Orion Nebula every 24 seconds to fill the Earth's oceans."

It's not hard to imagine, in other words, that Gliese 581g might have plenty of water as well. "It could have quite a good ocean," Vogt says. Certainly, it could be a sterile, nonbiological ocean. But unlike any planet found until now, there's nothing to rule out the idea that it could be teeming with life.

TIME Science Magazine Wed, September 29, 2010.

After intense scrutiny at multiple levels – none of the following pictures have been debunked by NASA or any other knowledgeable body.

Chichen-Itza, Mexico    **Washington DC, USA**

Apollo 15(1971) 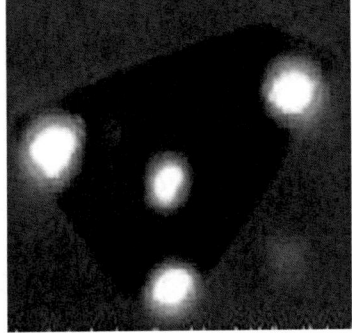   **Belgium**

This chapter was not put in to encourage you to spit in my face if our paths were ever to cross, for wasting your time or anything of the like. It is here to assist you with an interesting format of comment and conversation, if by chance you are ever lost of it in and of yourself. But mostly it is here so that you learn to question 'why?' in the things that you see fit – or unfit as the case may be.

CHAPTER 9   YOUR ROLE

Do as you would be done to – not unto others as they have done unto you. If each person in the world did their bit, we wouldn't have to worry about doing their bit for them. There'd be no street sweepers, because no one would be littering, no police – because well we'd all be doing our bit to prevent crimes not committing them. The world would just be one big unemployable place. But since the world holds no other greater guarantee than death, we know not everyone will do their bit and so others will continue to have to do more than their share to compensate for this.

Mother Nature is cleansing the earth in the form of what we call natural disasters. One after another she cleans until the earth is free from the damage we've done and the cycle again starts as it has done time and time again for millennia. As to Global Warming being a myth – just watch one documentary on TV about the Polar Bears and their diminishing icesheets and see what you think about the big GW then. Venice is sinking how much per year and there's no such thing as global warming. How so? What some declare as scare tactics – scientists now deem fit to agree, if we continue on in the way we have we will 'start a catastrophic chain reaction the likes of which we have never known'... or have we? The elements chain has already begun say some, and that we witness cyclones, floods and volcanic eruptions, fire and still dare say Nonsense to Global Warming is ideally non-sense in its truest form. Our children and our children's children are going to want to kick our a$$ when they find out that we knew this was happening and didn't do anything valid enough to stop it. 'There used to be trees lining streets and these things called tigers'...can you imagine what we have to tell our future generations, when we explain we let these creatures die out, and for the most part, we were entirely to blame for their absence and the privilege of seeing them alive.

Animals are reacting to us minimising their territories and food supplies; by eating us out of desperation and their limited options. We are perpetuating a disastrous cycle, increasing its intensity, we leave creatures no other option when we encroach on their space in such magnitudes. They will ultimately die out altogether and as the American Indian saying goes something like 'when all the birds are out of the sky & fish out of the sea, we will finally realise that money cannot be eaten' – and who do you think will be next. Really, who do you think will be next? How can there be a different outcome if we continue on in this same vein – our future is written in the clouds, the sea and the sands. The rainforest in Brazil diminishes by one & a half acres per second, yet there are cancer healing properties in these rainforests. We have lost more species in the last generation, than in the previous 65 million years. 19,817 species are extinct at the hands of man – starting from the Dodo Bird and we are losing approximately 200 species per day. Any scientist will tell you those statistics are alarming. AL-ARM-ING. Just remember if you continue to ignore, and not contribute 'your bit', once the damage is done; we cannot undo it and our fate will already be sealed. The adage "too little – too late" is going to mean more to us than it ever has. I'll be dead by then and so might you but your children and their children will not. If you won't do it for yourselves – do it for your future generations. Can you imagine what it will be like to grow up 20 years from now... if you don't have an equivalent of a Rhodes scholarship you won't be able to compete in the job market. University will be as commonplace as high schools so can you foresee the road of someone who doesn't continue on their studies; a hard and painful one. With the 5% contribution to cleaning up emissions by 2020 here in Australia – well hellava, what good's that going to do? They'll realise in 2020 that was never going to be enough. When grandchildren and their children grow up and hear tales long past, of trees and whales and gorillas... They will ask – "did you know? Did you know what you were doing to the planet?" and they will hold it against us. Do all you can to not contribute to the decline of the environment. And of course every one person can make a difference. It happens all the time. A mother who got a bill passed through Congress that instates a new law; which wasn't in place when her child was murdered because of the lack of it. Mother Teresa, Steve Jobs changed the world all but single-handedly. The list of examples spans across the oceans. You have much to offer – contribute.

If we all did no more than our part, our bit, then there'd be nothing left to do. For your souls journey = find out what your best 'bit' is to contribute and do your part to help. You will feel enriched by your contribution certainly. And if you've spent your life as a real sinner – consider it retribution, since you can't pay it back to a time long since passed, pay it forward - whoever's going to count your deeds at the end this should surely count for positives, one would think.

The thing about kindness, and genuinely kind acts, is it truly does give off that feeling in one's heart, the word to explain it you just can't put your finger on but you would recognise the feeling when. Life is a cycle. If you hold on tight and never give - the same is returned to you, you have to give out to get back but however, if that is really your only intention, then the good will of the heart is absent. You will not gain from that process, not long term anyways... But if you give freely and with love in your heart, you will be surprised how much good fortune comes of it. You join the cycle of life, of gift and gain. Try it. Another exercise if you're game - From this day forth – when someone asks you how you're doing – reply: "I'm livin' the dream" but smile and really mean it. Psychologically, you will be putting a new message into your conscious and subconscious mind, you will find – try it, all your actions and intents will steer you towards the things you seek most. Very successful people don't talk shiet on themselves, they dream big and don't dare for a moment contemplate the possibility of failure. Your mind will steer you towards the things you like most if you just direct and allow it. Paint the picture in your mind and feel and experience the emotions of having it already. Be grateful that it was given to you – it will come (still not the ex you want back).

Set your standards high, knowing that one evil deed does not make an evil deed response right. Lead by example in everything you do. Be the person people look at and aspire to be like. Revenge of any kind is an empty, hollow feeling, after the initial excitement wears off. Refrain from acts inducing just initial excitement.

Greater Positivity helps in every way, at every level of the physical and psyche. Consider the action required at this time or circumstance may call for 'inaction'. Remember when you're in a hole: stop digging.

Build up a toolbox to apply in emergency situations. From the cheating partner caught in action where your Plan B might be to say as little as you can, in a strong, soft tone and letting them come to you for damage control - to the knowledge of a completely boring subject, which may save the day in a lull at a party. Whatever it is; be prepared for the things that may come unexpectedly.

Life is a game although we are oft times told that this is not true. It's very similar with the characters and possessions you meet and collect along the way, that shape and form you into the person you become. Some people are masters of the game, some merely onlookers to life's game. If it is to be played well, treat your losses as you would as those in a game. Rarely cry about it when you lose; get on with your next move in a timely manner. You can't change losses however you can and do, move past them – albeit, sometimes it feels like it takes long to pass. But pass it does and we dust off and move along as expected we will. Very few things should make a permanent, long term impression on us. They should be things that were out of your control like death or disease of a loved one. If this is true in your case - Carry on your life in the manner that they would have wanted you to, not what you feel like going onward with. You owe them that homage and know that this is not all there is; and whether it's a brain chemical reaction or a near death experience – acknowledge there are those who have passed that threshold and in multiple accounts know upon their return, that death is nothing to be feared, it is just another milestone on your souls journey, of which your loved ones are never really far, regardless if their form lacks or contains matter.

Be ready to do the work and don't make a big song and dance about it. If they say,' there's 'no time like the present', which present is that? The day the guy first said it, the present of when the saying was made up... then everything is much overdue. There's no time like this present. Now is as good a time as any to start your changes.

We all want the best the world has to offer but do you even know what the best is? Is it relative to whether you prefer material things in life, electronic gadgets, the fancy car, or whether you are on a spiritual path and what wonders spirituality brings. We all have different versions of what the best things in life are. Understand that the best materialism has to offer, may not bring the best happiness has to offer and vice versa.

Live a well-rounded life engulfed in truth and good will and all else shall be at peace in your life. Be the upstanding pillar of the community you may have only heard about until now. Be all you can be. Ask yourself and then act on the question: **How best can I lead my life?**

> **A Native American grandparent was talking to their grandchild about how they felt about a tragedy. He said, "I feel as if I have two wolves fighting in my heart. One wolf is the vengeful, angry, violent one. The other wolf is the loving, compassionate one".** The grandchild asked them, "Which wolf will win the fight in your heart grandparent?". The grandparent answered, "The one I feed".

CHAPTER 10   THE ENIGMA

Sometimes you walk into a room and a person hasn't even glanced at you and 'you just don't like them' and other times you'll talk to a person for five minutes and feel like you've known them all your life. That's your vibe – the vibe you give off to others without ever knowing or intending. That's why sometimes in the office or wherever you might hear so&so's in a bad mood today and they haven't even spoken and you can just tell – 'you get the vibe'. They don't need to speak for you to know if they open their mouth it ain't gonna be good.

Most of it is natural – some people are genuinely kind, good souls and that light does shine through but know that it can be trained in the self just with an attitude change. When you are a good and kind person that flows over into everything you do; in all your acts and actions. That is your life and dang it feels good. Others see it and want it.

It is your responsibility to give off a good vibe and not walk around with the 'I'm a jacka$$' vibe to everyone you meet. No jokes – the world is enough without a shieta$$ poor mood so give it up, both for yourself and for those who pass your way. Not to mention how uncool it is – anger is about control. The more the loss (of control) the more the anger. Now that we're all on to you – knock it off if you are that way inclined. And if you are the victimised, you can act like it doesn't hurt when it does – that behaviour towards you is not ok; from anyone.

Practise the time worn strategies herein listed and have that essence of the enigmatic person we have all met at some point in our lives and admired, although we may never have known why and what was different that made them so. The Enigma is the calm, cool individual who under any circumstances seems in control and well controlled. They have a lightness about them that draws people to them like moths to a flame. A confidence that does not sway regardless of circumstance.

Positive and Confident in all they do, they have a natural ability to make one feel comfortable, important yet relaxed. It is readily apparent that the Enigma has the trappings of a strong, silent yet knowing vibe to them; people subconsciously know not to make them their fool. If you mimic the lessons herein contained you can have the impression of confidence and good self-worth. It will come to you in time. There are two sides to every person. The external side we expose to the everyday public persona and the private reality of who we really are, which moreover is absent for even family and spouses. Clean the internal so who your external shows is an upbeat, positive, confident being with a high awareness of self.

Enigmatic people are known for their spells of silence. This silence leaves room for another's own impressions. You hardly hear as much of how much damage has been done by not speaking, as opposed to what has been said. They make others know they have their shiet together in everything about them. That's not to say that when the lights go out at night the person that remains is the one with less than shreds of confidence (private reality). They travel or have another worldly air about them, which can be as simple as grace, charm or intellect.

CHAPTER 11   LIFE'S SECRET ELIXIR

Not Tested on Animals – Tested on Humans

Taken by Heads of Corporations - FORTUNE 500 COMPANIES

Heighten Memory & Motivation   Improve General Well-Being

All Natural   3 months' supply $29.95

Feel Remarkably Better than you have Ever Felt or your Money Back Guaranteed!

GUARANTEE ONLY ON THE CONDITION THAT YOU NEVER ORDER THIS PRODUCT AGAIN – YOU ARE NOT ALLOWED TO (because you will already know it works)

Now if I told you what I'm talking about is **Fish Oil pills. Krill or Calamari Pills** which have similar results. I have quadrupled the dose on myself over an extended period of time with no adverse reaction. Follow the recommended dosage after the first 3 months if you're doing the double dose boost, and see if you don't feel like you have just discovered life's secret elixir.

No, I don't sell it as it's readily available at any chemist or health food store so I don't need to. But if I just wrote 'take fish oil pills – they're amazing and noticeably good for you' - you could imagine how readily this advice would be disregarded.

CHAPTER 12   EPILOGUE

Teaching a child not to step on a caterpillar is as much benefit to the child as it is to the caterpillar.
                                                              MILLER

It doesn't matter which religion you belong – whether you call Jesus, Buddha, Mohammed, Allah or Whomever your God, what matters is that you know there is a higher being than you, whose behaviour you should aspire to and who loves and takes care of you. It is written that the Age of Aquarius is upon us and that these generations of children will grow up to protect the earth, its nature, and its creatures. Bindy and Bob Irwin are a perfect example of these Indigo-like children coming into place and thank heavens – we can't continue on in the greed rich vein of the 80's nor in the ridiculous expenditures of the 90's and 2000's. "People first, then money, then things" as financial advisor Suze Orman says. Get your behaviours in check and get on with the business of living the full and rich life you create for yourself. Find the person of your dreams and be the person you want to love you – that way you shouldn't put a foot wrong in your relationships whether as friends or more. If it's a friend – be the reliable, trustworthy friend you want. Really do unto others as you would want them to do unto you and that goes for all walks of life. Treat the supermarket checkout girl and the office cleaner as they are equals, as they are. Treat those in the higher echelons of life as if they still eat, shiet and sleep like the rest of us - They'll probably enjoy the change. Do you get it – this way of living doesn't cause you to toss and turn at night by actions made – it doesn't require the hard work of deceit or deception, your brain is more than twice as active when speaking deceptively versus how much thought process goes into speaking the truth. The truth is easy to remember, you don't forget the truth; and not the kind of truth – the 'no you don't look fat in that (chair)' – the kind of honesty that allows you to get a good peaceful night sleep without fear of any repercussions at morning's light. Harmony. It's when we lie or act in the negative that life becomes difficult. This is a harmonious path without taunt of those around you. Forgive what needs forgiving as and when you can; and move on from any toxic situation. You deserve that – treat yourself like you treat your lover, be good and kind to yourself. Have boundaries and limitations that cannot be trodden on and stick to them unless an extremely valid reason comes about, whereby you should consider these extenuating circumstances. Alcohol consumption by the way, is not an extenuating circumstance as alcohol is readily available, hence, as is then the chance of reoccurrence being high. Know that when you forgive an indiscretion of any nature it may very well be perceived as 'acceptable behaviour' by the forgiven as they have already seen the consequence is none. When you allow a person an action that is unacceptable to you, you are in essence saying it is alright. Even if you make them suffer a few weeks of not talking, they will know they just have to ride out your anger and they will be in the clear again. We really do train people how to treat us. You will undoubtedly sometime in the future face this same set of circumstances with the expectation of the same outcome. Be strong. Make room in the areas of your life you deem, at present, insufficient – leave open the opportunity for the right thing to be put in that place. It will come. It always does. Keep the faith.

Endeavour to have the true spirit of Christmas (or whatever your special holiday that brings out the best in you) year round. Be that kind, be that giving, be that person always. It sounds hard but in fact, it takes less negative energy, in time you'll come to see life's easier.

This is an overview of the tools you need, a guide or handbook if you will, not the whole solution itself – that will take time and work on your own behalf, and the subjects mentioned in here require investigation of your own, and to the degree you need/want to do it. There are many books on body language/talk language skills and reading the body and facial expressions – it is entirely up to you if you pursue it further than the information in this book. The "Get Your Game Up" training classes cover these areas in greater depth. The material herein should be enough to get you through a dinner party as a person of depth and forethought. There is much work required to get to the part where one feels whole in all aspects of life. Things that weren't in perspective before will now be easily assessed for importance. If you decide to follow the path of this book regardless to what degree, you will feel whole at the end – you will feel better than you have ever felt, just see how easy the flow of life becomes.

It is known, through the ages of visitations from Angels. They are painted as far back as our ancient ancestors carvings on rock walls. If I was to say Angels were real and they are around you when you need them – you just have to ask them for help, as they can't help you if you don't ask them for it. And say that there are people who believe in them worldwide who would readily tell you; they ask them for help all the time, for things so little as a good parking spot when they arrive at their destination… and these same people say they have a sense of peace with their problems, after they have enlisted the help of the angels, and the outcome is never as grim as it first appeared. If I was to say that in this book would you believe me? It doesn't matter, if you would or wouldn't – integrate this into your life as if it were true and see what you manifest.

Be the best you can be – and everything else will fall into place. Be the nicest/kindest person you can be, the most efficient at work giving all your focussed efforts to the company's goals and causes, respecting of all people and creatures, and the best things the world has to offer will come to you as a part of course.

When you are the best you can be in all aspects of your life – good things come to you, in bounty. The Right Way is the right way. It is also the easiest way. A path of goodwill will not go unrewarded. It is never too late to change your path. It only matters that you live a good and wholesome life, regardless at what point you decided to embark on that path. The change is the important part.

This is just the turning point on your journey, this day that you read the last page; make the decision to change for the better. The change is upon you -

DECLARE A NEW DAY

Bon Voyage

ASPIRE TO FULLFILLMENT – YOU CAN HAVE EVERYTHING THAT MAKES YOU COMPLETE.

Twenty years from now you will be more disappointed by the things that you didn't do than by the ones you did. So throw off the bowlines. Sail away from the safe harbor. Catch the trade winds in your sails. Explore. Dream. Discover. (Mark Twain)

When in doubt, Put Your Game Face On and play ball.

TRAINING SESSIONS: Bi-Annual

WEEKEND CRASH COURSE – (1 Day)
- Get Your Game Up
- Body Language
- Micro Facial Expressions/Reading Deception
- Self-Protection Strategies

INTENSIVE TRAINING COURSE – (3 Day)
Tailored to Corporate Needs
- The Art of Selling
- Sales Talk Language
- Sales Strategies / Customer Types
- Overcoming Objections / Closing the Sale
- Body Language
- Micro Facial Expressions/Reading Deception
- Get Your Game Up
- Tailored Corporate Manual
- Scripting Service (optional)
- Self-Protection Strategies (optional)

*Courses: 50% deposit at scheduling (hold dates available).
*Remaining 50% payable on course commencement
*Cancellation Fee 25% of Deposit monies.
*Rescheduling available (x2).

*Corporate Discount & Classes of 15 or more – 5% Discount entitlement.

Please direct all Enquiries via email to:
lotuscreativemgmt@outlook.com